SIMPLE CHURCH:
UNITY WITHIN DIVERSITY

SIMPLE CHURCH:
UNITY WITHIN DIVERSITY

ERIC CARPENTER, EDITOR

RedeemingPress.com

SIMPLE CHURCH:
Unity Within Diversity
© 2014 by Eric Carpenter

Published by Redeeming Press
Dallas, OR 97338
RedeemingPress.com

ISBN: 978-1-939992-28-4 (Paperback)
ISBN: 978-1-939992-29-1 (Mobi)
ISBN: 978-1-939992-30-7 (ePub)

"That they all may be one" is a petition
which in my prayers I never omit.
~C. S. Lewis

TABLE OF CONTENTS

Part 2: Living Radically

9

FOREWORD

Y ou hold in your hands a unique compilation of the insights of twenty-four different individuals chosen from across the world sharing what makes them passionate about the church of Jesus in the world. While each of these articles is unique and fascinating in its own way they harmonize in a glorious symphony of the ways Jesus wants to make His multifaceted-wisdom known in the world.

I love to read what makes someone's heart beat faster when they contemplate the reality of the Father's family taking shape in the world. By focusing on the positive side of church life, instead of where it's broken, many common themes emerge such as the supremacy of Christ, laying down our lives for others, handling Truth lightly so others can access Him even in their brokenness, and each of us learning to follow Him as we support and encourage each other.

Each of these contributors was chosen because they practice something called simple church. While definitions of that term may vary as does the way each of them lives it out, at its core simple church refers to people who are no longer engaged in institutional congregations that gather weekly.

Though many of them did so for multiple decades, each of them came to discover greater reality and freedom away from those structures and embrace the church as a family sharing His life together in homes, coffee shops, and anywhere else people naturally get together.

But even if you see the church differently than they do, you will find their heartbeat transcends simple church itself and strikes to the core of what it means to be God's children in the earth. You will find many people in more institutional settings that long for these same priorities and seek a church that reflects God as an endearing presence in the universe, inviting people everywhere into the reality of His life and truth.

I hope these themes become the fodder for conversations among His church, however they happen to gather. We need more conversation about these things, not less. And we need it not just with those who are like-minded, but even those who see things differently than we do but have the same heart for God and His kingdom.

This book is like a very long and very full buffet table as the contributors wrestle with the implications of doctrine, holiness, unity, giving and sharing. You'll want to devour it all, but you'll soon realize that there isn't enough time in the day or enough energy in the mind to live out all that's here. Just keep in mind that they are not talking about the church as an institution having to do all these things, or even as one individual doing them all.

They consider the church as a communion of persons, each part responding joyfully to the Head. It is enough to embrace the part He's given us as we encourage others around us to do the same. How He uniquely takes shape in each of us will make the glory of the whole far greater than the sum of its parts. We may not be able to do them all, but these don't dwell in the world of obligation. This is not how we have to live for Him, but how we get to live in His unfolding glory.

So take care not to reduce the table of contents into a list of objectives we have to achieve by our own effort. We couldn't even on our best day. What is described here is how Jesus takes shape in His church as each of us learns to live at His pleasure in this broken world. There will be strength enough, grace enough, courage enough, and wisdom enough for these priorities to shape the way we live. It is in learning to live in His love that we will be free enough to revel in His priorities and demonstrate His glory in the world.

This is His church to build and He does it well, often in mostly unseen ways. But she is taking shape in the world as He draws people together that share many of the passions outlined in these pages. May this book encourage your own journey and stimulate your passion to experience His life and share it freely with others.

~Wayne Jacobsen, author of
Finding Church: What If There Really Is Something More?
Newbury Park, CA

INTRODUCTION

Why write another book about the church? Aren't there enough already?

These are fair questions. Many, many books have indeed been penned that focus on church-related issues. Frankly, some of them appear to have been written just because the author wanted to write a book. Many books are written and published even though there's no need for them.

We decided to write *Simple Church: Unity Within Diversity* because we don't believe it has been written yet. We are a diverse group of twenty-four contributors who are, to varying degrees, engaged in simple church life. The purpose of this project is to write a book that is generally positive in tone and that tells what we believe. Instead of focusing on what's wrong with institutional Christianity, we desire to explain what we think the church can be and why.

This project began in the fall of 2013 after I wrote a blog post entitled "What I'm For." I had previously both read and written multiple blog posts blasting away at all sorts of easy targets within traditional Christian churches. This accomplished little. Therefore, I wanted to write something much more positive. Not long after I wrote that piece, fellow blogger Jeremy Myers from Redeeming Press suggested that we put a book together with that blog post as the foundation. This is what we did, with Redeeming Press as the publisher and me as editor.

The blog post contained twenty-five simple, positive statements such as, "I'm for a church that cherishes Jesus Christ above all things," "I'm for a church that is united in Christ," and "I'm for a church that is composed of peacemakers." These statements formed the table of contents. With a little tweaking here and there we had the backbone for our book.

Jeremy and I then invited a variety of Christians who are involved in simple church life to participate. Most of the contributors are bloggers since, obviously, bloggers like to write. Our contributors are diverse. While most live in the United States, some reside overseas. Even within the USA we live all over the place. Some contributors are male; some are female. Some are working, while others are retired. Most are white, but not all. Although we are all proponents of simple church practices, the local bodies we are a part of vary widely in both what they look like and how they function.

What we do all have in common is our Lord and Savior: Jesus Christ. We are all members of Christ's body. Because of this, we are united. In fact, we are all united with every other Christ-follower on earth, regardless of what we all believe about church life. This is because Christ's unifying of us is greater than any smaller differences between us. Reader, if you are in Christ, then Jesus has bonded us together.

In the end, unity within the body of Christ is what we hope to bring about through this book. Much misunderstanding currently exists within the larger body of Christ about what simple church practices are. Although all our contributors don't agree on everything, we do all hope that this book will generate positive discussion about church issues. We believe this text has the potential to be a starting point for positive dialogue among any groups of Christians. The more we understand each other, the more unity we can achieve, even if we disagree on significant topics.

As I said above, our intent was to compose a generally positive book. This does not mean that it is free of critique. Most of the contributors, myself included, see some very significant problems within institutional Christianity. If we didn't we would probably still be a part of traditional churches. As a former salaried pastor, I've seen up close many of the church issues that cause great problems for believers within institutional settings. What we do want to avoid in this book is the name-calling that is all too frequent in some sectors of those who have left traditional churches. While name-calling is harmful, healthy analysis can be beneficial.

When you look at the table of contents you'll see twenty-six chapters. Jeremy and I have each written two, while all the other contributors wrote one. This was not the original plan; it just worked out this way. As you read through this book, you will find that the various authors have written in different ways. Some focus more on in-depth Bible study, while others more on application. Regardless, all are grounded in Scripture, with at least some discussion of the daily outworking of the primary topic.

We segmented the book into five sections because that's how the topics worked out. They fit nicely into "Glorifying and Enjoying God," "Living Radically," "Building the Body," "Impacting the World," and "Proclaiming Salvation."

Please let me be clear on one more thing: simple church is not perfect. It's not perfect because it's made up of people. We all have our faults. All churches face their own struggles due to imperfect people trying to share life together. If we ever think we have this church thing figured out, then we've got a massive pride problem to deal with.

My hope and prayer is that God will use this little book to generate positive discussion about His church. If it helps even a few believers better understand simple church principles and practices, then I will be thrilled. We are not asking Christians to depart from institutional Christianity; rather, we just want to bring about increased understanding and unity.

Finally, I'd like to thank Jeremy Myers for both his idea of putting this book together and his willingness to publish it through Redeeming Press. I also want to thank all the contributors. Most have busy lives, yet nevertheless took time out to be a part of this project.

~Eric Carpenter, Editor
August 2014

Section 1

GLORIFYING AND ENJOYING GOD

{1}

A CHURCH THAT HONORS THE TRIUNE GOD

By Bobby Auner
Unless otherwise indicated, all Scripture references are from the ESV.

*He had prepared for you an abiding dwelling
with Himself, where your whole life and
every moment of it might be spent, where the
work of your daily life might be done, and
where all the while you might be enjoying
unbroken communion with Himself.*
~Andrew Murray

Wisdom begins in wonder. ~Socrates

I'm a city guy. I like living in the city. I like the noise. I like being around lots of people. I like the opportunities. Those who aren't big fans of city life can look at the very same things I appreciate about the city and consider those things to be demerits. The sights, sounds, and smells can sometimes be overwhelming. It all seems too busy, too distracting. Recently, I was reading about a man who had taken a trip to re-trace the steps of the first five books of the Bible. Along the way he spent quite a bit of time in empty desert locations. He noted that when most people think of the desert they usually assume it is quiet because there isn't a lot going on around you. Yet, he found that once he stepped foot on the land, the opposite was true. The desert is one of the loudest places you can be. Not because of the winds, but because of the stillness. It's loud because it's so quiet; every sound is magnified. Every vibration, every movement can be heard like it is being broadcast over a speaker. The soil crunches beneath the feet. A lizard scratches its way toward his destination. Tumbleweed rolls by. The wilderness has a way of emphasizing activity that would otherwise be ignored.

DELIGHTING IN THE DETAILS

This same principle applies in many aspects of life. A few years ago I began to see the church differently. I would look at the description of the *ekklesia* (the Greek word often translated as church) in the New Testament and then look at the organization I was a member of and see a huge disconnect. What I saw exemplified in the historical record of the 1st century *ekklesia* and what I was experiencing as "church" were worlds apart.

Just as a man traveled to the Middle East in order to retrace the footsteps of the first five books of the Bible, I wanted to experience fellowship with God and with my church family the way I saw it expressed in the Biblical texts. I wanted to embark on a lifelong journey that would honor our Triune God in all that I do.

God convicted me of playing church on Sunday. He gave me a burden for deeper relationships. He gave me discernment to see how the programs that I was involved with did little toward conveying spiritual life. I had a holy dissatisfaction with the mostly passive way I warmed a pew for most of my time together with other saints. Somewhere deep down inside I felt like I was being called out of comfortable rituals into a world of unknown possibilities.

After asking many questions of the leadership and becoming convinced that things were not going to change, I acted on my new-found convictions, as well as the request of the church leaders, and left the institution. Since that time I have learned to see and hear where God is working "outside the four walls." Just like the sound of tumbleweed in the desert, the wilderness has a way of emphasizing activity that would otherwise be ignored.

GOD CALLS, YOU GO

> Now the LORD said to Abram, "Go from your country and your kindred and your father's house to the land that I will show you" (Gen 12:1).

That's all you get, Abram. Leave what's well established and familiar and go. I'll show you where to go once you leave. If you faithfully obey there will be great rewards. When I put myself in his shoes, I realize Abraham isn't called the father of faith for nothing. It takes serious resolve to leave what's comfortable and lead your family into the empty harshness of the desert without knowing your destination. This is especially true when your only explanation for your actions is that God told you to, even if no one else has ears to hear His instruction.

In some ways it has been like that for our family. Once we were outside of the familiar surroundings of traditional Christian gatherings we realized the need to be spiritually-led people. We no longer had the rituals that kept us comfortably satisfied. Now there was a sense of the Lord leading us to something bigger, better, more glorious, more mysterious than we had ever experienced before. We were free, but free from what, for what, and to what? Those were the questions we now faced. The answers, it turns out, were much simpler than we ever thought possible. However, finding those answers meant facing some of our preconceived notions about familiar texts and re-examining them in light of God's leading. I'll give you one example to help you get a sense of what we faced.

CONFLICTING DIRECTIONS

> And let us consider how to stir up one another to love and good works, not neglecting to meet together, as is the habit of some, but encouraging one another, and all the more as you see the Day drawing near (Heb 10:24-25).

If you're like me you have likely heard this passage quoted numerous times as an instruction and even a warning to compel believers to regularly attend Sunday services. The author's words to the Hebrews haunted me while God began leading me away from the Sunday meetings I had always known. I remember praying, "God, I know you will not contradict your commands given in Scripture. So, what am I missing here?" I was in a very uncomfortable place. I wanted to be obedient to God but it seemed like God was commanding me to do something that directly contradicted the special revelation of the sacred texts. I knew there were only four possible reasons this could be.

1. I was listening to a deceiving spirit that was drawing me away from the church in disobedience to God.
2. The epistle to the Hebrews isn't inspired by God and therefore it does not carry His authority.

3. I misunderstood the promptings of God's Spirit.
4. I misunderstood the intended purpose and instruction of the text.

I'm sure you can imagine the conflict I was going through. This was a crisis of faith of the first order. I mean, regular attendance of the worship service is something that all obedient Christians must do in order to mature ... right? I supposed it was possible that I was under a delusion, but in what way was I deluded? Something had to give. Either the spiritual promptings were wrong, I could no longer trust the Bible as authoritative for faith and practice, or I had to challenge some long held interpretations of the text that have been passed down through generations of faithful believers. If God was really calling me to do something different then somehow the instructions I was spiritually discerning and the instructions of the text had to be in harmony.

Have you ever had that feeling in the pit of your stomach that comes when you've discovered something and you instantly know that the moment will change you forever? Perhaps you can recall the moment you realized your first child was on its way. Or, imagine how a child might feel after growing up in a family and discovering in his teens that he was adopted. Although he had no idea before, now that he *knows*, life will never be the same. In much the same way, part of me wished I could go back to my comfort zone before this conflict began. No matter how much I might wish for the bliss of ignorance, there was no choice. I had to go on.

CLOUD BY DAY, FIRE BY NIGHT

The greatest obstacle to discovery is not ignorance; it is the illusion of knowledge. ~Daniel J. Boorstin

I found myself regularly on my knees asking God to examine my heart and to lead me to the knowledge of His will. I had to find peace in this conflict because I knew that God is not the author of my confusion. I studied the Scriptures diligently and looked for clues as to what I was missing.

It turns out that what was missing was the form of the meetings I was accustomed to. Those forms were missing from the examples we have of the first century gatherings of believers. The Spirit of God brought me to passages of Scripture like Ephesians 4 and 1 Corinthians 14 and showed me what He desires an assembly to look like. Since none of the assemblies I had attended all my life resembled those exemplified in Scripture I realized God wasn't calling me away from obeying the instructions written to the Hebrews. To the contrary, God convicted me of my complacency in those forms that He hadn't ordained.

He led me out to learn to assemble with other believers in a way that allowed us to stir one another up and encourage each other as the command required. God was leading me toward obedience to the instructions and descriptions found in the post-ascension writings. There was no contradiction between the Spirit and the Scriptures. The confusion was because of the erroneous interpretation of the text that I inherited from other men. That meant I had to leave behind some well-established traditions and a lifestyle that was familiar and comfortable to me. I figured it was a small price to pay in order to follow God's lead into territory that was unpopular but held great promises. It was reminiscent of Israel's exodus from Egypt and subsequent wanderings in the wilderness.

AS YOU GO, MAKE DISCIPLES

With confidence in God's directing power through the Spirit, we can trust God to direct our steps as we learn to listen. As opportunities arise to encourage others, God is faithful in prompting us to stir them up in some way. We can simply ask the Lord for guidance throughout the day and trust Him to lead us into the works He had prepared beforehand for us to walk in. Only then can we truly understand through experience what it means to be a slave and to be free at the same time. This process aids us in realizing and confessing the impotence of our self-effort. Soon we are liberated from any inadequacies while being empowered by Christ's life working in and through us. The result is that God begins to possess us in the same way He possessed Christ. He will have His will performed in every way He desires. "For ye are bought with a price: therefore glorify God in your body, and in your spirit, which are God's" (1 Cor 6:20 KJV).

The whole of redemptive history is caught up with the purpose of establishing God's rule over all creation through God's people. It is about having His kingdom "on earth as it is in heaven" (Matt 6:10b). Do you realize the implications of that? Remember what happened when men were given spiritual vision into Heaven? Their mouths were silenced, their knees were weakened, they fell on their faces before the throne of the God. So mighty and awesome were the visions that their natural response was to prostrate themselves before Him and tremble. The angels offer praise to God continually by saying:

Holy, holy, holy, is the Lord God Almighty, who was and is and is to come! (Rev 4:8).

In doing so they are fulfilling the purpose for which they were made: to praise, honor, glorify, and magnify God with all that is within them. While in the presence of Divinity the sound of God's voice is overwhelmingly deafening. His Word accomplishes the purpose for which it goes out. A man who has been granted a glimpse of His majesty will be enrap-

29

tured by reverent awe and carry out whatever God has commanded with loving obedience. We should be rendered speechless before His peerless worth.

> I will bless the LORD at all times; his praise shall continually be in my mouth. My soul makes its boast in the LORD; let the humble hear and be glad. Oh, magnify the LORD with me, and let us exalt his name together! I sought the LORD, and he answered me and delivered me from all my fears. Those who look to him are radiant, and their faces shall never be ashamed (Ps 34:1-5).

IN SPIRIT AND IN TRUTH

As a result of spending time in the presence of the Lord our life will come from a new source, that of spiritual illumination in our innermost parts. Jesus told the woman at the well, "But the hour is coming, and is now here, when the true worshipers will worship the Father in spirit and truth, for the Father is seeking such people to worship him" (John 4:23). What I believe Jesus was teaching is that the old way of worshiping on this mountain or in that special place was becoming a thing of the past. God desires for true worshippers to worship in spirit and in reality. When Jesus ascended He promised to send His Spirit to remind us of Him and to keep Jesus at the forefront of our hearts and minds. Jesus promised, "I am with you always, to the end of the age" (Matt 28:20b).

This means we have very great and precious promises which guarantee us that as we walk in the Spirit, practice the remembrance of God's presence in our daily life, and seek to grow in the knowledge and understanding of the Lord Jesus Christ, all of life will become an act of worship. Our life will be a testimony to the faithfulness and steadfast love of our Father in Heaven. Our acts will manifest our Lord and Savior Jesus Christ as an organic expression of his indwelling life. Our energy will be the power of the Holy Spirit in and through us as we enjoy constant fellowship with one another and with the Father and the Son. As a result we will be an assembly of living sacrifices, devoted to honoring our Triune God in all aspects of life.

{2}

A CHURCH THAT CHERISHES JESUS CHRIST ABOVE ALL

By Edwin Aldrich
Unless otherwise indicated, all Scripture references are from the NLT.

*Don't store up treasures here on earth,
where moths eat them and rust destroys
them, and where thieves break in and steal.
Store your treasures in heaven, where moths
and rust cannot destroy, and thieves do not
break in and steal. Wherever your treasure
is, there the desires of your heart will also be
(Matt 6:19-21).*

A little more than a decade ago, my wife and I were blessed with our first child, a beautiful little girl. For her first Christmas, I purchased a small stuffed dog from the jewelry store where I was working security and placed it on the edge of her crib. The next morning when we came to her room, the dog had been pulled down into the crib, and she was happily chewing on the ear of the stuffed animal. That little stuffed dog and our daughter quickly became inseparable. Everywhere the one went, the other was sure to be. Our daughter became dependent on the little dog toy to fall asleep or to calm her when she was upset or sick. Ten years later, our now tween-aged daughter still sleeps with her "Dog Dog." Although the toy dog looks much worse for wear and has lost most of its stuffing, she still refuses to take trips away from home without it.

When I think of what it means to "cherish" or treasure something, one of the first things I think of is my daughter and her little stuffed dog. Of all the stuffed animals she has owned, many much larger, newer, and prettier, this one little dog holds a special place in her heart that no other thing could usurp. This little toy dog has been with her through so much and has been part of so many memories my daughter has stored up that it has become treasured in a way that transcends its actual or intrinsic value.

Someone observing my daughter interact with this toy dog could easily tell that she places an extraordinary value on it. In the same way, we can take clues from people's words and actions which tell us what it is that they consider valuable. One example would be sports teams; a man who places a lot of value on a particular football team will often wear clothes with the team colors or logo. When you talk with that person, he might tell you all the statistics about the players on his team, or about how many games that team has won. In fact, with many committed sports fans, it is impossible to spend much time watching them or talking to them without finding out which team they support. When you go away from the conversation, you might say something like, "Wow, this guy really loves football," or "Wow, this guy really loves the Dallas Cowboys."

When looking at a group of people or an organization, like a church, we can use the same observational patterns to determine what they consider to be valuable. For instance, a church may consider evangelism to be the most important part of their organization; therefore, they will regularly hold revival meetings or evangelistic campaigns. When you spend a little time talking to a member of that church, you may notice that they focus on making sure that people have heard their evangelistic message. In the same way that a child cherishes a special toy, or a sports fan cherishes their favorite team, observing the behaviors of a church tells much about what the church cherishes.

WHAT A CHURCH TREASURES

Since "cherishing" or treasuring an object quite literally means to give additional value or importance to an object, we run into one particular difficulty: how to measure or identify that additional value. In imagining what a church that cherishes Jesus above all else might look like, I have chosen to look at four areas that help us to "measure" or identify those things upon which a church might place additional value.

1. How a church looks
2. How a church acts
3. How a church speaks
4. How a church invests

When a church cherishes Jesus Christ above all things, people who encounter how that church body looks, acts, speaks, or invests will go away saying something like, "Wow, that church really loves Jesus."

HOW A CHURCH LOOKS

When we place value on something, it affects our appearance. Let's look again at the football fan; he wears his team's colors or logo on his clothes. Sometimes, on the day of a game, he will paint his face or dye his hair with the team's colors. It is important for this fan that people recognize which team he is supporting, and his appearance is a large part of conveying that message.

God makes it clear in the Bible how important he considers outward appearances. When the prophet Isaiah foretells the coming of Jesus he says, "There was nothing beautiful or majestic about his appearance, nothing to attract us to him" (Isa 53:2b). Jesus himself even criticized the religious leaders of his day by saying, "What sorrow awaits you teachers of religious law and you Pharisees. Hypocrites! For you are like whitewashed tombs—beautiful on the outside but filled on the inside with dead people's bones and all sorts of impurity" (Matt 23:27). So how would a church that cherishes Jesus Christ look? Would everyone dress nicely, or look clean cut? Would the building be nice and new and shiny? Would they have the best music and the most comfortable chairs or the most dynamic speakers? What do we know about Jesus' outward appearance and what people saw when they looked at Him?

We can draw a clue from one of my favorite stories in the Bible, found in John 8. The religious leaders bring a woman to Jesus who was caught in the very act of adultery. They demand that He give the righteous condemnation she deserves. Instead, Jesus says, "Go ahead, you who have never sinned throw stones at her." This crowd, which was ready to carry out the death sentence on the woman, departs until only Jesus and the woman are left. Then Jesus asks the woman, "Where are those who accuse you and would condemn you?" The woman looks at Jesus and says there is no one.

The Pharisees expected Jesus to condemn this woman. He would have been completely just to do so; however, when she looks at Jesus, she already knows that there is no one left to condemn her. Jesus confirms this and says that He does not condemn her either, but she already knew it, just from looking at Him. Oh that people could come into our churches, regardless of their lifestyle or sin condition, and we could ask them that same question, "Where are those who would condemn you?" Then we would know that people see in us the same love and acceptance that Jesus displayed.

HOW A CHURCH ACTS

One common accusation leveled against churches is that the people are hypocrites, meaning that they claim to believe something but act in a way that is inconsistent with those beliefs. Like the old cliché says, our actions speak louder than our words. In the case of the church, people are paying attention to see if our words and actions truly matchup. Jesus Himself called the religious leaders hypocrites numerous times. In fact, in Matthew 6 Jesus warned His followers not to practice their religion outwardly to be seen of men, as the hypocritical leaders did, but rather to do their good deeds where no one could see them.

As a church that treasures Jesus Christ, how would we honor Jesus' words regarding how we act? A lot of churches start by asking the question, "What Would Jesus Do?" In fact, this has become almost a cliché in churches today; people wear T-shirts and jewelry and write books and spend many hours trying to guess what Jesus would do in certain situations. This speculation about what Jesus might do or not do has led to many disagreements about what Jesus would be like. I am convinced that churches need to ask a slightly different question. Perhaps, instead of, "What would Jesus do?"

we can simply ask, "What did Jesus do?" We have the example of Jesus, and while He was not necessarily faced with every possible situation we will be faced with, we can look at how He lived and try to do the things He did. Jesus healed the sick, fed the hungry, and had compassion on the lost. He took time to teach children, and spent time ministering to tax collectors and prostitutes. He rebuked the religious leaders for burdening people with their rules and taught freedom and life. A church that values Jesus Christ worries less about trying to figure out what Jesus would do and instead focuses on trying to do what Jesus did do.

HOW A CHURCH SPEAKS

While it is true that our actions speak louder than our words, our words are still valuable in demonstrating what things are important to us. By nature, we like to talk about the things that are interesting to us. If you spend a little time talking to a person, it is not difficult to determine what they consider important. For example, when you talk to bikers you will learn what brand of motorcycle they prefer, what models they like and don't like, what size engine they have, what accessories they have or want, and so on.

As Christians, we have become particularly adept at speaking Christian-ese. We know what words other believers expect us to say. Often we say them not because we actually believe them, but because it is expected. We say things like, "God is good, all the time" and "God bless you." One of my personal favorites is, "I will be praying for you." There is nothing wrong with any of these phrases, in and of themselves; however, rarely when we say, "God bless you" do we really mean, "I am asking God to bless you." It is more like a hello or goodbye in Christian-ese. Rarely when we say, "I will be praying for you" do we really mean that I will spend considerable time this week interceding for you before God. Most often we mean something more like, "I really don't want to be troubled with your problem right now, so I say that I will pray and be absolved of any further responsibility to assist you with your problems."

As an avid biker, when I envision the church that cherishes Jesus Christ, I tend to think about people who cherish their motorcycles. Just like we discussed in the above paragraph, it is difficult to come away from a conversation with the motorcycle enthusiast without at least a good idea of what they cherish. The conversationalist may say something like, "Wow, that guy really likes *Harley Davidson* motorcycles" or "that guy really loves his Dyna low rider." Similarly, when a person spends time in conversation with a church that cherishes Jesus, they should come away saying something like, "Wow, those people really love Jesus." You could not have a conversation with such a church and be left wondering where the treasure of their heart is.

HOW A CHURCH INVESTS

This is one of the most telling things about what a person considers to be most valuable. The things that we have to invest—time and money—are both limited, meaning that we only have so much of them available to us. Because of this, we must make a value decision every time we choose to spend time or money. Whether consciously or unconsciously, each time we spend money, we declare which thing is more valuable to us. Someone who spends a lot of money on nice clothes values their appearance and what others think about them. These decisions are not necessarily good or bad, but they reveal a lot about what is important. They can also be an indicator of a larger problem. For instance, spending money on alcohol and not having enough to eat or pay rent can be an indicator of a problem with alcoholism.

Churches, in much the same way, also have limited resources. Churches only have a finite amount of time and money to spend. Where and how we choose to spend or invest those resources speaks a lot about how we prioritize. In the first letter to Timothy, Paul gives this instruction, "Teach those who are rich in this world not to be proud and not to trust in their money, which is so unreliable. Their trust should be in God, who richly gives us all we need for our enjoyment. Tell them to use their money to do good. They should be rich in good works and generous to those in need, always being ready to share with others. By doing this they will be storing up their treasure as a good foundation for the future so that they may experience true life" (1 Tim 6:17-19).

Is a building necessarily a bad thing? No. Is paying a salary to a pastor or church staff necessarily bad? No. Is having entertaining music or comfortable chairs or a great speaker bad? No. None of these things taken alone are bad. In fact, they all can be used for the kingdom of God, but they also can be used to build man's kingdom.

A church that treasures and values Christ invests its time and money in the things that were important to Jesus Himself:

All the nations will be gathered in his presence, and he will separate the people as a shepherd separates the sheep from the goats. He will place the sheep at his right hand and the goats at his left.

Then the King will say to those on his right, "Come, you who are blessed by my Father, inherit the Kingdom prepared for you from the creation of the world. For I was hungry, and you fed me. I was thirsty, and you gave me a drink. I was a stranger, and you invited me into your home. I was naked, and you gave me clothing. I was sick, and you cared for me. I was in prison, and you visited me."

Then these righteous ones will reply, "Lord, when did we ever see you hungry and feed you? Or thirsty and give you something to drink? Or a stranger and show you hospitality? Or naked and give you clothing? When did we ever see you sick or in prison and visit you?"

And the King will say, "I tell you the truth, when you did it to one of the least of these my brothers and sisters, you were doing it to me!"

Then the King will turn to those on the left and say, "Away with you, you cursed ones, into the eternal fire prepared for the devil and his demons. For I was hungry, and you didn't feed me. I was thirsty, and you didn't give me a drink. I was a stranger, and you didn't invite me into your home. I was naked, and you didn't give me clothing. I was sick and in prison, and you didn't visit me."

Then they will reply, "Lord, when did we ever see you hungry or thirsty or a stranger or naked or sick or in prison, and not help you?"

And he will answer, "I tell you the truth, when you refused to help the least of these my brothers and sisters, you were refusing to help me."

And they will go away into eternal punishment, but the righteous will go into eternal life" (Matt 25:32-46).

Much debate exists about the above passage. I am still not sure I am certain who the sheep or goats in the parable are. However, there is one thing in this parable that I am not able to get away from: the Lord Himself identifies with the poor, the naked, the hungry, the sick, and the imprisoned. In fact, He calls these people His brethren. He so identifies with them that how we treat them is inextricably linked to how we are treating God. I don't really need to fully understand this story to know that it gives us a glimpse into just how important the poor and the hungry and the sick and the broken are to God. When we show kindness to the least of these, we are doing it to God. Conversely, when we fail to love the least of these, we also are failing to love God. Is there grace for our failures? Yes, there absolutely is, but if we are seeking to treasure Jesus, we should also be seeking to love who and what He loves.

CONCLUSION

Ultimately, this is not about a list of things that we need to do or not do in order to be a "good" church. Clearly, we will talk about some things besides just Jesus, and we will not all dress or act the same. We may not all like the same people and we may not all give our money to the same causes. I do not believe that it was ever God's desire for all Christians to look the same or talk the same or even act the same. God created the world, and He also created the diversity and individuality we see all around us. Ultimately I believe it is God's desire for His church that when people see us and listen to us they cannot help but recognize that, "Those guys really love Jesus." That is the goal: to treasure Jesus Christ so much that people cannot help but recognize that it is love for Jesus above all other things that drive us to do what we do.

{3}

A CHURCH THAT
FOLLOWS THE LEAD OF
THE HOLY SPIRIT

By Chris Jefferies
Unless otherwise indicated, all Scripture references are from the NIV.

Jesus sent His Spirit to be with us always and to guide us. Whether we think in terms of the church as a whole, as a local body of believers, or as a collection of individuals, the church must pay attention to the Holy Spirit. Eight points help clarify and justify this statement.

JESUS IS THE WORD

First of all, *Jesus is the Word in bodily form* (John 1:14). He came from the Father who actively sent Him (John 6:38). He came as Redeemer to find the lost (Luke 15:1-7). He came as High Priest (Heb 4:14) and offered Himself as the sacrificial Lamb (John 1:29).

43

THE CHURCH IS CHRIST'S BODY

Secondly, *the church is Christ's body and is composed of His people* (1 Cor 12:27). The church as body applies at every scale, from two people in relationship with one another and with Christ (Matt 18:20), through the typical small group of twelve to twenty, through local gatherings (Rom 16:5), trans-local groups (Acts 9:31), and on to national scale and beyond. Church is not defined in terms of size, organization, structure, hierarchy, or tradition; it's built on the knowledge of who Jesus really is (Matt 16:16-18) and it depends upon His presence among His gathered and interacting people. The church is a living temple (2 Cor 6:16; 1 Pet 2:5), the Bride of the Lamb (Rev 21:9), and will one day be made perfect in every way.

JESUS SENDS THE SPIRIT

Thirdly, *Jesus sends the Holy Spirit.* When He returned to the Father He sent the Holy Spirit (the set-apart Spirit, the Spirit of Christ, John 15:26). Christ said He would remain with us (Heb 13:5; Matt 28:20).

THE CHURCH RECEIVES THE SPIRIT

The fourth point is that *the church must receive the Holy Spirit corporately and individually.* He is our advocate, explainer, leader into the whole truth, and representative of the Father and the Son (John 15:26). The individuals who form the church receive the Spirit individually. But He also manifests Himself when we meet together (1 Cor 14:26-40). If we fail to receive the Spirit of Christ we fail to receive Christ Himself.

44

THE SPIRIT CHANGES AND EMPOWERS THE CHURCH

And fifth, *the Spirit changes us and empowers us.* There is the growing fruit of the Spirit—love, joy, peace, patience, kindness, goodness, faithfulness, gentleness, and self-control (Gal 5:22-23). And there are also the equipping gifts of the Spirit—apostle, prophet, evangelist, shepherd, and teacher (Eph 4:11-12), along with many ministry gifts. We need both, individually and together. If we were allowed only one it had better be fruit because fruit is foundational. Fruit is about character; gifts are about power. Any of the gifts without the fruit would be an abomination. Imagine, if you can, a shepherd with no love, an apostle with no self-control, or a teacher with no patience. And the fruit in the absence of the gifts might lead to a helpless church full of good intentions. Power without character is dangerous, while character without power is less effective.

The Holy Spirit is the Spirit of Christ the Son, and of the Father who sent the Son. We can never succeed, individually or as the church, without all that the Spirit has for us, the fruit and the gifts, character and power together. Without these the church cannot go forward. We need nothing more but can get by with nothing less as Jesus builds His church.

THE SPIRIT IS LIFE

The sixth point is that *the Spirit is life* (He is breath, a wind that blows any way He pleases; the breath gives life). We begin as dry and disconnected bones, and we are built into a complete body. Without the Spirit we are not alive and cannot fulfill Father's purpose for us (Ezek 37:1-14).

THE SPIRIT IS NECESSARY

The seventh point is that *without the Holy Spirit we can do nothing*. Jesus said, "Apart from me you can do nothing" (John 15:5). He also said that when He returned to the Father He would send an advocate, the Holy Spirit (John 14:16-17). Paul refers to the Spirit as the Spirit of Christ (Rom 8:9), so in a sense it must be true that without the Spirit we can do nothing. At any rate, without the Spirit of Christ we can only do what humans can do, which in the great scheme of things is not very much.

THE SPIRIT SENDS THE CHURCH

And finally, *the Holy Spirit is a sending Spirit*. Isaiah 61 is fundamentally about the coming of Messiah, but the chapter is also about us as we go in His Name. Read these words and make them your own! Jesus is the "Sent One," but He has also sent us. We are His witnesses (Acts 1:8).

THE SPIRIT IN ACTION

The eight points listed above can be illustrated by how the Holy Spirit has led my family and me over the past several decades.

In the mid-1970s I was caught up in the Charismatic Movement that swept through the church at that time. It was an exciting few years! My first wife, Judy, and I had recently bought our first house and had pre-school daughters. We were from an evangelical free church background where the accepted teaching was that the gifts of the Spirit were no longer active in the church.

But reading the Bible for ourselves, and especially the New Testament, we could see no reason not to expect gifts such as tongues, prophecy, healing, and the rest. So when we met people from other denominations who had come to the same conclusion, we began to get together regularly in full expectation that we would receive what had been promised. And we were not disappointed! First, our friend Tony began speaking in a tongue while he was having a bath. After this, we were all released into a variety of gifts. The meetings were enriched by visions, prophetic words, wisdom and knowledge, and prayer for healing. We even prayed for a noisy central heating pump that had disrupted some meetings in our home, and it became (and remained) obediently quiet.

We read widely, listened to recorded messages from well-known speakers, sang all the new songs, went to meetings and rallies to hear the big names, studied the Bible avidly, and continued to meet in our homes every week. But it didn't last. After some years of these glory days, people got involved in a variety of other activities and separated out over doctrinal or other issues. Some settled back into denominational life, some into the new streams of charismatic church that were developing. Most of us wanted to build something, forgetting that Jesus said, 'I will build my church'. Were we listening to the Spirit in this? Were we being obedient? What might have happened if we'd continued to follow what He was showing us?

A FRESH START

Years later, when our daughters were finishing school, Judy became ill with cancer. We invited some of our close friends from those early days to come and pray with us. We were all astonished when we began to meet and pray; once again, the Holy Spirit rested among us and upon us in ways we could never have imagined. We had some of the most amazing and awesome times of praise and worship I have ever experienced. Jesus took us on a deep spiritual journey and revealed Himself and the Father to us through the presence of the Spirit. We learned such a lot about Him and about one another. It was a time of emotional and spiritual healing for all of us.

Judy, however, was not healed of the cancer. It took its course and she died late in 1995. She knew she was dying yet it didn't seem like a defeat to either of us. Rather it was a victory over death of a kind we could never have imagined. The two girls are now happily married with children of their own while I have remarried. Donna and I live near Cambridge, and I am still on a spiritual journey.

The reason I share all this is that we discovered for ourselves that the Holy Spirit is both necessary and sufficient for church life. Without Him we will be helpless no matter what we add in the way of teaching, study, organization, structure, or tradition. But if we have the Spirit and add all these things anyway we will find we have added nothing fundamental. Indeed, much that we add may get in the way. The Holy Spirit will say, "Do such and such." Instead of just doing it, we may think we were not taught to do it, or it's against our traditions, or it doesn't fit our policy or our mission statement.

We learned by simple experience that Jesus and His Spirit will lead us into everything He wants us to do. This knowledge has stayed with me throughout my life. My advice: don't add anything and don't take anything away. Jesus gave us a commission to make disciples and a command to love, but He did not ask us to build His church.

GOING FORWARD TODAY

Returning to the story, Donna is a member of Open Door Church, part of the New Frontiers group of churches. I am not a member, but I am involved in several ways, especially as part of Donna's Small Group. However, I also meet regularly with a variety of other friends for prayer and Bible study and to listen to what the Spirit shows us. I'm involved with other folk socially, as well; we meet for coffee and in other ways. I know that in sharing my own life with them, I am also sharing something of Jesus' life, too. After all, He lives within me, has given me a new heart of flesh and has filled me with the presence of His Spirit. Wherever I go, and whoever I'm with, the Holy Spirit is there, too.

I now want to represent Christ in everything I do. I want to be salt and light in an often broken world. He's still teaching me how to do this, and I still keep messing things up. But He doesn't seem fazed by even the very worst I can do. Why? The answer to that is often summed up in the word "grace." Paul Young expresses it more fully when he says, "It's not about what we do, it's about who He is." In other words, the Father's love and acceptance and approval of me are not dependent on my actions, but on His character and nature. Surely this is the attitude we should have towards other people; we should be known for our gentle acceptance.

Some of the highlights recently have centered on living life as His child. People I have been reading and listening to include Alan Hirsch, Neil Cole, Felicity Dale, Paul Young, Steve Addison, and Michael Frost. There is purity and wholeness in walking with the One who is pure and whole in every way. A precious goal for me is to become ever more like Him in the way I treat the people I meet daily. I know that I need a heart that is like His and that it's a matter of growing in the fruit of His Spirit.

SOME IMPORTANT PRINCIPLES

Can we distill some principles from all of this? There are several, and I believe they are hugely important.

The Holy Spirit teaches us to be more like Christ. His fruit builds in our lives over time. He equips us by pouring out His gifts as and when they are needed. He builds us in relationship. The Holy Spirit sends us out on mission. He wants us to live in the world as a blessing and a challenge. He is always doing new things.

When we meet, the Spirit meets with us. After all, Jesus lives in each one of us, and the Holy Spirit fills us to overflowing. Usually that overflowing serves to inform our meetings, guide our thoughts, lift our hearts into the presence of the Most High, and speak to us moment by moment in our lives. The Spirit prompts this one to sing a particular song, that one to share some verses from the Bible, another to pray in a tongue, and yet another to interpret. One person tells us about something that happened during the week, another one brings a prophecy. And through these gifts we serve one another so that together we all receive the full picture. That picture always resembles Christ.

This is normal church life when we meet together, just as Paul describes it in 1 Corinthians 12-14 and Ephesians 4. And meeting like that is far more rewarding and encouraging than any human wisdom or knowledge or music could ever be. Be joyful in all you do. Rejoice in Christ! Rejoice that you are in Him and He is in you! Rejoice that you are free and alive and filled with His Spirit. Francis Chan, speaking at Verge 2013 said this.

God says "Rejoice in the Lord always, I say again rejoice"... I want you to rejoice, I want you to rejoice in the Lord. *I* want to rejoice in the Lord. I want this to be a *time* of joy. Because remember who we are ... God put His Holy Spirit inside of us. We're temples of the Living God, we're children of God. Almighty God is up there in heaven looking at us, His adopted children, that He thought about before the creation of the world! And we can't walk around with this lack of joy, that's not what He wants for His kids. He wants us so blown away by His truths that with great joy we proceed [through life].

What would church be like without the Spirit? It's quite hard to imagine. I wonder if it could even be called "church" at all! Church without the Spirit of Christ? I don't think so!

{4}

A CHURCH THAT CLINGS
TO SCRIPTURAL TRUTH

By Steve Scott
Unless otherwise indicated, all Scripture references are from the NASB

We're for a church that clings to Scriptural truth—in all aspects of life. At first glance this statement seems to have quite a large scope. *All* aspects of life? When we look at what this means we see that it has to be an ongoing pursuit; a pursuit that grows and matures. Indeed our pursuit of this will continue our entire lives.

A church that believes it should hold to Scriptural truth in such a way must first understand what the church is—and what it is not. It must understand what the church does—and what its limitations are. It must understand its place in God's Kingdom. It must understand what happens within the church—and what can and does happen outside the church. It must understand what it has authority to do—and what it is forbidden to do.

WHAT THE CHURCH IS

The church (Gk., *ekklesia*) is primarily an assembly, or if one prefers, an assembly of ones who are called out. We believe this is what the New Testament has in mind when we read of the church. I won't belabor the definition here, as many books and online resources are readily available.

The New Testament paints several metaphors for us regarding how the church is related to Christ. One is that the church is like a bride and Christ like the bridegroom. Another is that the church is like a body with Christ like the head. A passage that connects these two themes is found in the epistle of Ephesians:

> So husbands ought also to love their own wives as their own bodies. He who loves his own wife loves himself; for no one ever hated his own flesh, but nourishes and cherishes it, just as Christ also does the church, because we are members of His body. For this reason a man shall leave his father and mother and shall be joined to his wife, and the two shall become one flesh. This mystery is great; but I am speaking with reference to Christ and the church (Eph 5:28-32).

The apostle Paul also uses the body metaphor to indicate how we relate to each other, "For just as we have many members in one body and all the members do not have the same function, so we, who are many, are one body in Christ, and individually members of one another" (Rom 12:4-5), and, "For even as the body is one and yet has many members, and all the members of the body, though they are many, are one body, so also is Christ" (1 Cor 12:12). He connects Christ to the body in this fashion, "He is also head of the body, the church; and He is the beginning, the first-born from the dead;

so that He Himself might come to have first place in everything" (Col 1:18). The church, of which we are all members, has Christ as its head, and we are members of one another. Paul expounds on the metaphor with some body dynamics, "… and not holding fast to the head, from whom the entire body, being supplied and held together by the joints and ligaments, grows with a growth which is from God" (Col 2:19).

So far we have a basic description of what the church is. It is the bride of Christ. It is the body of Christ, with members being members of one another, held together by joints and ligaments, and is caused to grow by God Himself. We're for a church that looks like the body metaphor used in Scripture.

What the Church is Not

It is just as important for the church to know what it is not as it is to know what it is. All the aspects of life and functions in life are part of the Kingdom of God, yet all are not part of the church. All are not governed by the church or administered by the church. The church is not my family, although in a sense it is the family of God. The church is not my employer or other source of living, although there are those who are employed by their church. The church is not the civil magistrate or the military. Although the church is involved in teaching, the church is not the source of all education. The church is not a medical research facility, a health club, a kids' soccer league, or the fire department.

Equally important, the church is not a group of other popular notions. It is not a building, although a building a church meets in is commonly called a church. It is not a social club, although there is a social aspect to the church. It is not a political or business bureaucracy. It is not a program run by a charity. And it is not a legal status granted by a civil government. We're for a church that knows what it is not.

WHAT THE CHURCH DOES

The most obvious function of the church, since it is an assembly, it that it assembles! It does a number of other things when it assembles as a body. "And they were continually devoting themselves to the apostles' teaching and to fellowship, to the breaking of bread and to prayer" (Acts 2:42). These are bedrock, foundational functions of the church. A church which devotes itself to these things as common practice could be called "an Acts 2:42 church."

The church also holds up truth for the world to see. As Paul writes, "I am writing these things to you, hoping to come to you before long; but in case I am delayed, I write so that you will know how one ought to conduct himself in the household of God, which is the church of the living God, the pillar and support of the truth" (1 Tim 3:14-15). The church lives out what it shows the world.

The church recognizes the individual gifts given to each believer:

> For just as we have many members in one body and all the members do not have the same function, so we, who are many, are one body in Christ, and individually members of one another. And since we have gifts that differ according to the grace given to us, let each exercise them accordingly: if prophesy, according to the proportion of his faith; if service, in his serving; or he who teaches, in his teaching; or he who exhorts, in his exhortation; he who gives, with liberality; he who leads, with diligence; he who shows mercy, with cheerfulness (Rom 12:4-8).

The church not only does that, but also recognizes the people themselves with those gifts: "And He gave some as apostles, and some as prophets, and some as evangelists, and

56

some as pastors and teachers" (Eph 4:11), with the goal of building itself up in love (Eph 4:16). We should recognize those whom God has gifted and be content and confident that their gifts will be put to good use. After all, we are the ones who stand to benefit from the gifts of others. On the other hand, the apostle Paul has something to say to us about those that are either not obviously gifted nor have a strong position in life or in the church:

> On the contrary, it is much truer that the members of the body which seem to be weaker are necessary; and those members of the body, which we deem less honorable, on these we bestow more abundant honor, and our unseemly members come to have more abundant seemliness, whereas our seemly members have no need of it (1 Cor 12:22-24a).

Giving attention to the celebrities and accomplished people in life is the way the world works. But here we are told to actually give more honor to those who are naturally less honorable. Do we in the church practice this? I have seen it in action in a profound way within an assembly, and it is a great encouragement to those who receive honor. Only recently has medical science come to understand the importance of a seemingly inert part of the human body, the appendix. Once thought removable, we now understand important functions it has had all along. What Paul is essentially telling us is that God will bring out things in others we didn't know were there if we only honor them! This way, we will all have the same care for one another (1 Cor 12:25), and nobody will be left out. This is a great facet of our unity in Christ.

One thing to notice in the New Testament with regard to how we should function in the church is that most of our directives are in how we relate to one another and not how we relate to structure or program. Whatever structure or program we adopt, we should continually review what we do to see if relating to one another is being hindered. Do we have a program that cannot honor the least among us? Let us revise that program to include them! Do we have a structure that can deny a believer the legitimate use of their gifts? Let us revise the structure! We're for a church that puts our relation to others in a position of fulfilling Scriptural truth.

The church does many other things including preaching the Gospel to those outside, caring for widows, eating the Lord's Supper, and all the many other things I have not listed here. All of what the church does combined, as a body, constitutes a very important task in our relationship to Christ. It is the church as the bride readying herself for her groom, Christ (Rev 19:7).

LIMITATIONS OF THE CHURCH

The first limitation we need to realize is that the church is not the Kingdom. The Kingdom is much larger than the church. What the church is not, as I outlined above, should give us food for thought in deciding which areas of life it will not govern. The church may have teachers who help people live their lives outside the church, but the church itself will not control that.

Church leadership also has limitations. Its pastors/elders are admonished by Peter to "... shepherd the flock of God among you ... nor yet as lording it over those allotted to your charge, but proving to be examples to the flock" (1 Pet 5:2-3). Shepherds should never control, manipulate, dictate, or make their own rules about other people's lives, but should serve as examples for others to follow. We all appreciate somebody who walks the walk, getting their hands dirty along with us more than somebody who dictates to us from a corner office with a view. We're for a church that knows its limitations.

KINGDOM > CHURCH

This point must be reiterated: the Kingdom is much larger than the church. When members of the church understand this, it can pave a way for great service to others. The church can also encourage its members to engage others outside of our own meetings. We have a great number of people all around us who we can minister to, including many believers who attend different churches than we do. We are commanded to love our neighbor as our self. This is such a high priority with God that is called the second Great Commandment.

As an example of how this can be done, my family was able to help out a friend (a single dad who attended a different church) through participation in youth sports. We offered to sign his son up for youth baseball, and with the league's approval to let him play on our son's team, we were able to take him to all the games and practices. It truly bought joy to the family, as the dad was able to see his son play in a few games, and the boy had the time of his life. We were also given the opportunity to follow through on commitment, as our son broke his thumb a couple of games into the season! We still made all the practices and games, with our son being the unofficial bat boy. It also helped to bring our families closer together.

ALL ASPECTS OF LIFE WILL APPEAR IN YOUR CHURCH

We can be certain that if we are a church that clings to Scriptural truth in all aspects of life, then all aspects of life will appear in our church. People's lives are complex, and many aspects of life overlap or even collide. The church will need to help its members deal with those complexities, all the while recognizing its limitations. One of the most difficult (yet most wonderful at the same time) limitations of the church is the not knowing how Scripture applies to some situations. The Bible simply doesn't speak to everything we will encounter in life (Rom 11:33). Like Job, we sometimes will simply have to rest in knowing that God is in control.

Likewise in the church, we will encounter people who have different beliefs than we do. How this is dealt with may be complex. We may not know how to resolve all differences and simply allow another the liberty of believing before God. Scriptural truth can be dim and cloudy to us, as Peter testifies that many of Paul's words were difficult to understand (2 Pet 3:16). But we can persevere in prayer and in love of God and in love of our brothers and sisters. "The conclusion, when all has been heard, is: fear God and keep His commandments, because this applies to every person" (Eccl 12:13). We're for a church that clings to Scriptural truth in all aspects of life.

{5}

A CHURCH THAT HOLDS THEOLOGICAL CONVICTIONS WITH HUMILITY

By Chuck McKnight
Unless otherwise indicated, all Scripture references are from the NET Bible.

Finally, all of you, have unity of mind, sympathy, brotherly love, a tender heart, and a humble mind (1 Pet 3:8, ESV).

Few matters have created greater division in the body of Christ than theology. And I'm talking about more than bad theology—good theology can be just as divisive. Of course, theology itself is not really at fault. The problem lies in how we hold to our theology. We desperately need humility.

Theology is a fancy word used to describe the things we believe about God. Since we all believe something about God, we all have a theology. And that makes everyone—from pastor to atheist—a theologian. I certainly would not propose giving up on theology, even if that were possible. Nor would

I suggest accepting everything we hear, being "carried about by every wind of teaching" (Eph 4:14). Theology is as important as it is inescapable. Our picture of God shapes the way we live. God revealed truths about Himself through Scripture, and I believe He wants us to learn about Him and what He has planned. More importantly, He wants us to change into the image of His Son as a result of our studies.

Some concepts in the Bible are straightforward, and few people dispute them. Other concepts are so confusing that few even claim to understand them. Between such extremes are a range of ideas that seem obvious to some but not so obvious to others. We ought to be studying the Bible and learning more about God, but what happens when we disagree? Unfortunately, most Christians throughout history have chosen one of two prideful responses—either separating over their beliefs or persecuting those who believe differently. Even more unfortunate is the fact that this still happens in the church today.

This raises some questions. Is it ever right to separate over theology? If so, when? How can we hold to theological convictions humbly without causing division? Before we can examine these questions, we need to grasp the importance of unity in the body of Christ.

HOW IMPORTANT IS UNITY?

Unity has been referred to as a "first tier" doctrine.[1] It is one of the core teachings that God Himself is most concerned with. The theme of unity runs throughout the New Testament, but for the sake of brevity, we will focus on one key passage.

---

[1] I borrow this phrase from Alan Knox, who is another contributor to this book. Alan Knox, "Unity a 'first tier' doctrine?" *The Assembling of the Church*, April 15, 2010, accessed January 16, 2014, http://www.alan knox.net/2010/04/unity-a-first-tier-doctrine/.

What follows are the words of Jesus, spoken to God the Father on the night of His arrest.

> I am no longer in the world, but they are in the world, and I am coming to you. Holy Father, keep them safe in your name that you have given me, so that they may be one just as we are one. ...
>
> I am not praying only on their behalf, but also on behalf of those who believe in me through their testimony, that they will all be one, just as you, Father, are in me and I am in you. I pray that they will be in us, so that the world will believe that you sent me.
>
> The glory you gave to me I have given to them, that they may be one just as we are one—I in them and you in me—that they may be completely one, so that the world will know that you sent me, and you have loved them just as you have loved me (John 17:11, 20-23).

Several important truths about unity should be noted from this passage.

First, Jesus prayed that His followers would be unified to the same extent that God the Father is unified with the Son. The inseparable union of Jesus with His Father is what He wants us to have with one another.

Second, our unity is not only with one another, but also with Jesus and with the Father. Jesus is in us, while we are in Him, while He is in the Father, while the Father is in Him, while we are in the Father, while the Father is in us. So when we separate from fellow believers, our division actually affects the unity of the Godhead.

Third, the unity of believers is intended as a primary reason for the world to believe in Jesus. Our unity is supposed to prove God's love. Is it any wonder that unbelievers scoff at a Christ whose followers are so divided?

SHOULD WE DEFEND CORRECT THEOLOGY?

When believers separate over theology, it is usually because one or both sides think the other's theology is so wrong that they cannot remain in fellowship. As justification for this divisive behavior, they often appeal to verses that talk about "sound doctrine" or "heresy." Of course, both groups pridefully imagine that they are protectors of sound doctrine but that the other group promotes heresy. This approach has caused the majority of schisms and persecutions throughout church history. It also reveals a misunderstanding of both sound doctrine and heresy as spoken of in the Bible.

The term *sound doctrine*, when used today, typically refers to correct theology. And the word *heresy*, in today's language, usually refers to a dangerously wrong theology that goes against standard Christian teaching. So when we read such terms in the Bible, we tend to assume they refer to correct or incorrect theology. In reality, these Biblical terms have little to do with theology at all.

The Greek behind *sound doctrine* literally means "healthy teaching."[2] While such teaching can potentially include theology, it is primarily used to prescribe actions. Thus Paul's list of things "contrary to sound teaching" is composed entirely of immoral lifestyles—not one is a false theological con-

---

[2] For further discussion about "sound doctrine" vs. "healthy teaching," see the following two articles, written by other contributors to this book: Jeremy Myers, "Preach the Word—2 Timothy 4:2," *Till He Comes*, September 09, 2011, accessed January 16, 2014, http://www.tillhecomes. org/preach-the-word-2-timothy-4_2/ and Keith Giles, "What is 'Sound Doctrine'?," *Subversive1*, July 26, 2011, accessed January 16, 2014, http://subversive1.blogspot.com/2011/07/what-is-sound-doctrine.html.

cept (1 Tim 1:9-10). And again, in Paul's qualifications for an overseer, "so that he will be able to give exhortation in such healthy teaching and correct those who speak against it," every item is a matter of lifestyle, not theological accuracy (Titus 1:7-9).

As for *heresy*, it comes from the Greek *hairesis*, which means a "division." Similarly, the word for *heretic* means a "divisive person." So when Paul instructed Titus to reject a heretic, he meant to reject anyone set on creating disunity. Even then, the heretic was to be given two chances to repent from his divisive ways (Titus 3:10). Heresy, as Biblically defined, is not a matter of wrong theology. Even correct theology can be heresy when used divisively. Division itself is the heresy warned about in the Bible. And sound doctrine— though very important—is a matter of how we live, not what we believe.

IS THEOLOGY EVER WORTH DIVIDING OVER?

We have seen that Jesus considers the unity of His followers to be essential. We have also seen that traditional excuses for division lack Biblical support. The Bible never allows for division among believers over matters of theology. However, it does instruct us to separate from false teachers (who are not true believers at all).

If we are to be thoroughly Biblical, we must limit our criteria for false teachers to that which the Bible explicitly condemns. They are to be identified primarily by their lifestyles (see Matt 7:15-20 and 2 Pet 2:14-19); however, they may also be revealed as false teachers by proclaiming a different Jesus. The Bible does indicate that a few theological belief statements are non-negotiable components of the Gospel and thus worth separating over. By my count, there are only five of them:

- Jesus is the Messiah, the Son of God (Matt 16:16-18; John 20:31; 1 John 2:22-24; 5:1).[3]
- Jesus came to earth in the flesh (1 John 4:1-3).
- Jesus is a descendant of David (2 Tim 2:8).
- Jesus died for our sins, was buried, and was raised on the third day (1 Cor 15:1-4).
- Jesus is Lord (Rom 10:9; 1 Cor 12:3; Phil 2:11).[4]

All five points, stated multiple times throughout the New Testament, are summarized and labeled as the "Gospel" in the beginning of Paul's epistle to the Romans.

This Gospel he promised beforehand through his prophets in the holy Scriptures, concerning his Son who was a descendant of David with reference to the flesh, who was appointed the Son-of-God-in-power according to the Holy Spirit by the resurrection from the dead, Jesus Christ our Lord (Rom 1:2-4).

Of this Gospel, Paul wrote that "even if we or an angel from heaven should preach to you a Gospel contrary to the one we preached to you, let him be accursed. As we have said before, so now I say again: If anyone is preaching to you a Gospel contrary to the one you received, let him be accursed" (Gal 1:8-9, ESV). So yes, we should distance ourselves from those who claim the name of Jesus while teaching a false Gospel. But such people are not truly believers—thus our unity is not compromised. Furthermore, if some individuals misunderstand the Gospel while not teaching others likewise,

---

[3] It could be argued that this point consists of two separate beliefs; however, I have chosen to represent them as one statement because they are so frequently listed together in the Bible.

[4] Note that many of the cited passages cover multiple of these five belief statements. I simply chose not to repeat references.

there is ample room to simply show them from Scripture what they have missed.

While this may make a provision to separate from some people, it is actually far more inclusive toward fellow believers than any "statement of faith" I'm aware of. Most belief statements serve only to cause division over secondary matters of interpretation and opinion. But in the Bible, I can find no beliefs that justify division apart from these five. We have been commanded to remain united, regardless of what some of us may believe about Scripture, creation, salvation, justification, baptism, spiritual gifts, God's sovereignty, man's free will, end times, heaven, hell, or any other pedantic excuse for separation.

> Now may the God of endurance and comfort give you unity with one another in accordance with Christ Jesus, so that together you may with one voice glorify the God and Father of our Lord Jesus Christ.
>
> Receive one another, then, just as Christ also received you, to God's glory (Rom 15:5-7).

Why—given that the Bible so explicitly forbids it—have we so consistently chosen to divide over theology? The answer, quite simply, is a matter of pride.

HOW CAN WE HOLD THEOLOGICAL CONVICTIONS WITH HUMILITY?

Our own pride turns theology into a matter of division. We pridefully assume that our own theological grounding—whichever camp we happened to be born or converted into—is the version that finally got it all right. Or we pridefully suppose that our own intelligence or ability to study and interpret is of a greater quality than others. Pride makes us so certain of our own rightness that we're willing to divide over beliefs. This pride flies in the face of our duty as believers.

> Therefore, if there is any encouragement in Christ, any comfort provided by love, any fellowship in the Spirit, any affection or mercy, complete my joy and be of the same mind, by having the same love, being united in spirit, and having one purpose. Instead of being motivated by selfish ambition or vanity, each of you should, in humility, be moved to treat one another as more important than yourself (Phil 2:1-3).

Paul instructed us to "be of the same mind." This does not mean having exactly the same theology. Rather, it means sharing a singular focus. We should be so fixed on the "one purpose"—Jesus Christ—that nothing else can become a reason for division. Paul further instructed, "Treat one another as more important than yourself." A more literal translation renders it, "Considering one another better than yourselves" (LEB). In other words, give others the benefit of the doubt. Assume they have good reasons for disagreeing on some point of theology. Our unity is far more important than determining who is right and who is wrong.

At this point, I feel I should reiterate something I said earlier. I do not advocate a lazy anything-goes approach to theology. Theology is important. We are right to study the Bible. It is good to hold convictions about what we believe. And it is certainly appropriate to discuss theology with fellow believers. But it must be done humbly. Here are a few suggestions for maintaining humility while discussing theology:

1. Realize that you are wrong. All of us are—no exceptions. You may not be wrong about everything, but you certainly aren't right about everything either. Since you're guar-

anteed to be wrong about some things, you still have more to learn.

2. Learn how to learn from others. I've found that I often gain the most from those with whom I most strongly disagree. God gifted us all differently, and that includes our areas of understanding. If you're convinced a fellow believer is wrong in one area, you probably have a lot to learn from that person in other areas.

3. Make every effort to understand differing viewpoints rather than trying to disprove them. You can't truly understand a belief by reading a book written against it—such efforts rarely represent the other side accurately. Instead, try getting to know people who hold different beliefs. Ask them personally for explanations. Don't defend your own beliefs; just listen.

4. Seek the truth together. Ignore the desire to prove your theology. If your current beliefs are wrong, you should want them to be corrected. If they are right, they will hold up without your defense. Winning a debate doesn't prove a theology, but debates can tend to polarize people away from each other. Be ready to explain your beliefs when others ask, but be even more ready to listen as others give their explanations.

5. Remember that you are part of a family. If you would not separate from a family member over theology (and I certainly hope you wouldn't), remember that your union in the family of God is far more important than that of any physical relation. We are brothers and sisters in Christ, and there is no reason we can't agree to disagree.

6. Keep your eyes on Jesus. When He is the focus, little else matters. Determine, along with Paul, "to be concerned about nothing … except Jesus Christ, and him crucified" (1 Cor 2:2).

WHAT AM I FOR?

I'm for a church of individuals who hold theological convictions with humility. I'm for a church that receives all brothers and sisters, just as Christ received them. I'm for a church that values theological diversity. I'm for a church that would never think of dividing over theological opinions. I'm for a church that needs no statement of faith as a source of unity, because it is fully united around Jesus Christ.

> I, therefore, the prisoner for the Lord, urge you to live worthily of the calling with which you have been called, with all humility and gentleness, with patience, bearing with one another in love, making every effort to keep the unity of the Spirit in the bond of peace (Eph 4:1-3).

Section 2

LIVING
RADICALLY

{6}

A CHURCH THAT IS MOST NOTABLE FOR ITS LOVE

By Sam Riviera
Unless otherwise indicated, all Scripture references are from the NIV.

We want to be known as a church that is most notable for its love. If we do not love our neighbors, does anything else we might be known for have any meaning? For most people it does not.

But who is our neighbor? What does it mean to love our neighbor as ourselves? Who better to answer those questions than Jesus Himself? He did exactly that in the story of the Good Samaritan, found in Luke 10:25-37.

THE GOOD SAMARITAN

I love the story of the Good Samaritan. The story is often called a parable, a story told to illustrate a lesson or truth. I think Jesus told the story of an actual event, perhaps one with which his hearers were familiar. However, whether He relat-

73

ed an actual event, or merely told the story, He used the story to teach truth.

Jesus chose a Samaritan to be an example to not only his Jewish listeners, which included at least one religious expert, but also to all of us who follow Him. A Samaritan undoubtedly seemed a strange choice to Jesus' listeners.

The expert in the law who attempted to test Jesus asked Him, "What must I do to inherit eternal life?" When Jesus in turn asked him, "What is written in the Law?" he answered, "Love the Lord your God with all your heart and with all your soul and with all your strength and with all your mind" and "Love your neighbor as yourself."

Jesus told the expert in the law that he had answered correctly. "But he wanted to justify himself, so he asked Jesus, 'And who is my neighbor?'"

In reply Jesus told him the story of a man traveling from Jerusalem to Jericho who was robbed, beaten, and left for dead by the side of the road. A Jewish priest passed by and ignored him. A Levite, who assisted the priests in their duties, also saw the man. He too passed by on the other side of the road. The priest and the Levite were probably on their way to Jerusalem to perform their religious duties in the Temple.

Later a Samaritan happened by. He too saw the injured man. But he did not pass by on the other side. He bound up the traveler's wounds, took him to an inn, and cared for him. He even made arrangements for the innkeeper to look after the man, promising to pay the bill when he returned.

After telling the story, Jesus asked the expert in the law which of the three he thought was a neighbor to the man who had been robbed and beaten. The expert in the law replied, "The one who had mercy on him." Apparently he couldn't bring himself to say "the Samaritan."

Jews hated Samaritans, foreigners whom the Jews considered to be descendants of settlers that the Assyrians had brought to Samaria from other lands they had conquered.

Their religion was wrong. Even though they supposedly worshipped the right God, they worshipped Him in the wrong way and in the wrong place.

Would not any Jew know that a Samaritan could not possibly be capable of loving his neighbor as himself, regardless of the nationality or religion of the traveler? Nevertheless, Jesus chose a story about a Samaritan both to illustrate who is a neighbor and to give an example of how anyone, even a Samaritan, might love his neighbor.

MODERN DAY SAMARITANS

Is it possible that we the church can learn not only from Jesus' story about a beaten traveler who was taken care of by a Samaritan, but also from some modern day Samaritans? I believe we can, based on the stories of two brothers who didn't appear to have the correct religious beliefs. Yet those two men knew how to be a neighbor to someone in need.

Harold and Frank were "rough around the edges." They swore constantly. They didn't swear like a sailor. Their swearing could make even a crusty sailor blush. Stories circulated about their escapades, stories I won't repeat. Maybe the stories were true, maybe not.

I slightly knew Frank and Harold, but my father was the center of my life. I couldn't imagine life without him as a part of it.

The unimaginable happened. My family discovered that my father had a terminal illness. A week later he died. I was devastated and felt that I had been left half dead by the side of "my road."

I remember almost nothing about his funeral except that it was held in the largest church in the area, since everyone in our small town and most of the people in the surrounding

75

towns knew and loved my father. Hundreds of people filled the church.

Before, during, and after the funeral, most of the people from our church vanished. They never noticed me lying by the side of the road. The pastor never said anything to me about my father dying, never ever. Neither did most of the people from church.

Were they too busy with life to check with me and see how I was doing? Were they too busy to talk to me, to spend time with me, to care? Did they not know what to say?—I will never know.

The day after my father's funeral, Harold, a man who knew my father and ran a business down the street from my father's business, called me on the phone. He said, "Sam, I know your dad told you about my coin collection. I took part of it out of the bank vault to catalogue and I thought you might like to see it this evening. I have to take it back to the bank tomorrow morning."

I went over to Harold's house that evening, where Harold and I looked at a fortune in gold and silver coins. We talked about coins and about coin and gun shows. At the end of the evening, Harold asked me if I would join him that Sunday on a trip to a coin and gun show.

"I know you go to church, and I don't want you to miss that. What time does it get out?"

"About noon."

"I'll be parked around the corner, waiting for you."

I slipped out during the last prayer. Harold and I were speeding down the road on the way to the coin and gun show before anyone else came out the church door.

Harold and I attended many coin and gun shows over the next several years, until I graduated from high school and went away to college. On our rides there and back, and sometimes at Harold's business and home, we discussed just about everything.

Harold trusted me completely and I trusted him. When we attended the coin and gun shows, Harold usually had me carry his bag. I knew he had money in the bag, money he used to buy coins. One time we got separated at a large show for about an hour. When I found Harold he told me that he was starting to get worried about me.

"Do you know what's in that bag I gave you to carry?"

"I never looked, but I think it's money."

"That's right. I figured no one would try to rob you, thinking a kid wouldn't have anything in there worth stealing."

On our way home from the shows, we always stopped at Harold's favorite bar. Harold went in. I stayed in the car.

"Don't worry, Sam. I'll have just one beer, and then we'll go home."

A couple of minutes after Harold went into the bar he always emerged with a soda and a bag of chips for me, then returned to the bar. Ten or fifteen minutes later, he was finished with his beer and we went home.

I had enough sense not to mention to my mother the bags of cash that Harold gave me to carry and our regular stops at the bar. However, it never occurred to me until after Harold had died that perhaps Harold used poor judgment in those areas. At the time, I didn't see poor judgment. I saw someone who cared about me, took me into his life, and trusted me implicitly.

Harold's brother Frank was cut from the same cloth as Harold. Frank lived a few houses down the street from me. Rumor had it that Frank was even coarser and meaner than Harold.

Frank always had time to talk. I walked and rode my bicycle past his house. Frank always stopped what he was doing to talk to me. He showed me all of his tools and explained how they worked. He occasionally hired me to go help him with his construction business.

Frank helped me with repairs on our house. He and I painted the house. He charged us $35 for about three days of work, knowing that was all we could afford.

Even though they believed in God and were "God-fearing men", neither Harold nor Frank were what most of us would call Christians. Good church people avoided the likes of them and told me so. I didn't care. They loved me and showed it by what they did. The good church people had other things to do, things that didn't involve a hurting teenager.

Frank and Harold mellowed considerably in their old age. Most people eventually figured out that the foul language, stories, and crusty exteriors were just bluster. They figured out what I had found out long before - Harold and Frank were really a couple of softies. In the last years of his life, Frank became a Christian, a pillar of his church.

WHAT CAN THE CHURCH LEARN FROM SAMARITANS?

Did God really rob me of my father? These days I don't understand it that way. However, I did when my father died, and I felt like I'd been robbed and left half dead by the side of the road. The priests and the Levites passed me by and pretended not to notice. But a couple of Samaritans, guys whose religion was either lacking or wrong, picked me up, bound up my wounds and took care of me.

Who is our neighbor? Just as with the Samaritan in Jesus' story and just as with the two brothers in my story, it can be whomever we happen across in our journey of life, as well as whoever happens across us.

How will we notice that our neighbor has been beaten up by life and left half dead by the side of the road? Pass by on their side and take time to notice.

What should we do when we find such people? Be their neighbor. Stop. Bind up their wounds. Be their friend. Do whatever we can to help them in a practical way. That is called love.

Why should we help them? They probably got themselves in the mess they're in. Jesus tells us to help them. Listen to Him.

But they are _____ (fill in the blank: addicts, alcoholics, prostitutes, stinky, filthy, undeserving, gay, morally corrupt and many other things). The traveler in Jesus' story needed help, not based on his religion, morality, financial status or any of the things we use to judge others. Jesus explained that the Samaritan helped the traveler, and then Jesus told the expert in the law, "Go and do likewise." Luke tells us the story so that we religious folks will understand that Jesus is also telling us, "Go and do likewise."

As part of the church, I feel love toward the unfortunate. But I don't have the time or money to help them out. Jesus said nothing about whether the Samaritan had the time or money. Jesus told us that he did not pass by the beaten man, but stopped, bound up his wounds and took care of him. Jesus said, "Go and do likewise."

Does this work? It worked for me. Without Harold and Frank I probably would have lost my faith in God.

LEARN TO LOVE OUR NEIGHBORS

We the church can learn to love our neighbors. As Jesus' story of the Good Samaritan and as the stories of the two brothers illustrate, sometimes we may even learn this story from people we wouldn't expect.

We want to be known as a church that is most notable for its love for its neighbors, for those the church happens across, and for those who happen across the church. We want to be known as a church that helps others in practical ways, even if

SIMPLE CHURCH: UNITY WITHIN DIVERSITY

we think they may not deserve help. This is the Gospel in action. This looks like Jesus.

{7}

A CHURCH THAT
FORGIVES

By Eric Carpenter
Unless otherwise indicated, all Scripture references are from the ESV.

*Then Peter came up and said to Him, "Lord,
how often will my brother sin against me,
and I forgive him? As many as seven times?"
Jesus said to him, "I do not say to you seven
times, but seventy-seven times"
(Matt 18:21-22).*

Former tennis star John McEnroe was known as much for his on-court temper tantrums as he was for his athletic skill. When upset over a perceived poor call by a referee, McEnroe would famously yell, "You cannot be serious!"

When I read certain Bible passages my first reaction is occasionally similar to McEnroe's. While I'm not angry, I still want to complain to God, saying, "You cannot be serious!" Matthew 18:21-22 is one of those passages. The reason is that it seems impossible. And it is—at least apart from God. This is because forgiveness is supernatural. It is not of this world. In fact, forgiving someone flies in the face of all this world stands for.

Our sin-saturated world lives according to a perversion of the eye-for-an-eye principle. Revenge is the norm. This, of course, takes a wide variety of forms, but it basically boils down to getting back at someone for something they did to you. The idea of forgiving them, of refusing to retaliate, of actively forgetting what they have done is absolutely nonsensical to those living according to a fleshly worldview.

God demands and desires that His people be forgivers. His church must be composed of people who, because their hearts have been regenerated, actively live lives of forgiveness. If there is one place where forgiveness should be the norm it is Christ's body.

Where did this other-worldly concept called forgiveness even come from?

FORGIVENESS BEGINS IN THE CHARACTER OF GOD HIMSELF

The Scriptures tell us a great deal about God. Some of the most important passages are those in which God describes Himself. Exodus 34:4-8 is one of those passages:

> So Moses cut two tablets of stone like the first. And he rose early in the morning and went up on Mount Sinai, as the Lord had commanded him, and took in his hand two tablets of stone. The Lord descended in the cloud and stood with him there, and proclaimed the name of the Lord. The Lord passed before him and proclaimed, "The Lord, the Lord, a God merciful and gracious, slow to anger, and abounding in steadfast love and faithfulness, keeping steadfast love for

thousands, forgiving iniquity and transgression and sin, but who will by no means clear the guilty, visiting the iniquity of the fathers on the children and the children's children, to the third and the fourth generation." And Moses quickly bowed his head toward the earth and worshiped.

It's important for us to see just how God describes Himself. If anyone knows God perfectly, it is God. Among other things, God says that He is "merciful and gracious," "slow to anger," "abounding in steadfast love," and "forgiving iniquity and transgression and sin." These are key attributes of God. They do not waver. For the purposes of this chapter, we must note that God is forgiving of sin. *It lies in His very character.*

The last part of the above passage shows us that God responds differently to those who repent and those who do not. However, it is clear that God in no way withholds forgiveness from those who genuinely seek it. Why? Because He in His essence is a forgiving God.

He is also a God who forgives completely. The Lord does not hold back in any way. Psalm 103:12 informs us, "As far as the east is from the west, so far does He remove our transgressions from us."

Some of us no doubt have a tendency to partially forgive. We do so grudgingly because we know we're supposed to. We don't forget. We still treat the offending person differently because our forgiveness is not 100%. God's forgiveness is 100%. It is perfect. It is complete. It lacks nothing.

JESUS CHRIST: THE MAN OF FORGIVENESS

Our Lord and Savior Jesus Christ was many wonderful things. One of those things was a man of forgiveness. He both taught it and lived it.

In the Bible, Jesus' first major teaching passage falls in Matthew chapters 5-7, what we refer to as the Sermon on the Mount. In these chapters Jesus focuses on His expectations for His people. His teachings, quite simply, turn the world on its head. He says things that are truly radical. In Matthew 5:38-48 Jesus challenges the world's faulty understanding of the eye-for-an-eye principle. He tells His listeners that His disciples will not retaliate and will, in fact, love their enemies. They will forgive instead of fighting back. This must have been stunning to the crowd. Frankly, it is still difficult to believe today. I don't have any personal enemies in my life. However, if I did I would struggle to forgive and love them.

In Matthew chapter six Jesus again turns to forgiveness. Mentioning it as part of the Lord's Prayer, He then elaborates on it, saying, "For if you forgive others their trespasses, your heavenly Father will also forgive you, but if you do not forgive others their trespasses, neither will your Father forgive your trespasses" (6:14-15). We see a connection, then, between God's willingness to forgive us and our forgiveness of others.

Jesus further explains the relationship between our forgiveness of other people and God's forgiving of us in the parable of the unforgiving servant (Matt 18:21-35). This is the passage where Jesus instructs Peter that he must be willing to forgive seventy-seven times (symbolic language for limitless forgiveness). In this parable we see that God's forgiveness of us is infinitely more significant than any forgiveness we can give to another person. However, if we fail to forgive it is a sign that we do not truly know God. If this is the case then we will not be forgiven.

These are some very challenging words from Jesus. They wouldn't be worth believing if Jesus didn't live it out. After all, if no one can actually forgive this way then what's the point? Jesus talked the talk, but could He walk the walk?

In a word: Yes.

If anyone ever put-His-money-where-His-mouth-is it was Jesus Christ. We all know the account of His arrest, "trials," scourging, crucifixion, and death. Isaiah tells us that Jesus was disfigured to the point that He no longer looked human (52:14). Christ's crucifixion was the ultimate act of selflessness because it was the ultimate act of suffering—and by the only person who never deserved it. Jesus not only suffered physically, but also spiritually. The sinless lamb became sin (2 Cor 5:21). In the midst of this unimaginable torture Jesus prays, "Father, forgive them, for they know not what they do" (Luke 23:34).

If I'd been hanging there on a cross I likely would have been cursing my executioners, happy that they would probably be cast into Hell someday. Jesus instead asks His Father for their forgiveness even as He perishes. Amazing.

Our Lord, who is both our sacrifice and our model, was a man of forgiveness. Karl Barth once said:

> Look once again to Jesus Christ in His death upon the cross. Look and try to understand that what He did and suffered, He did and suffered for you, for me, for us all. He carried our sin, our captivity and our suffering, and did not carry it in vain. He carried it away.

FORGIVENESS IS AT THE HEART OF THE GOSPEL

The Gospel is the good news of Jesus Christ. It is the message that we can be in a right relationship with God Himself. This wonderful news is made possible by the sacrificial death of Jesus Christ on the cross. Because of what the Son of God accomplished we can be forgiven our sins.

I hope we never get over the truth that the perfect, all-powerful God is willing to forgive our sins. This is at the very

85

SIMPLE CHURCH: UNITY WITHIN DIVERSITY

heart of the Gospel. Because Christ has paid it, we don't have to. If we will repent and believe, we will be saved.

The importance of personal forgiveness does not begin in the New Testament. We see it throughout the Bible. For example, Psalm 32:1 tells us, "Blessed is the one whose transgression is forgiven, whose sin is covered." In the book of Isaiah we read, "Come now, let us reason together, says the Lord: though your sins are like scarlet, they shall be white as snow; though they are red like crimson, they shall become like wool" (1:18).

On the night before Jesus was crucified He took a cup and told His disciples, "Drink of it, all of you, for this is My blood of the covenant which is poured out for many for the forgiveness of sins" (Matt 26:27-28).

This theme of forgiveness flows along wherever the Gospel is proclaimed. Again and again we see it as the good news spreads out in the book of Acts. In Acts 2:38, just after the Holy Spirit has descended, Peter preaches, "Repent and be baptized every one of you in the name of Jesus Christ for the forgiveness of your sins, and you will receive the gift of the Holy Spirit." We see forgiveness in Acts 5:31, 8:22, 10:43, 13:38, and 26:18.

The epistles are also full of forgiveness. For example, Paul writes, "In Him we have redemption through His blood, the forgiveness of our trespasses, according to the riches of His grace" (Eph 1:7). John echoes this, saying, "If we confess our sins, He is faithful and just to forgive us our sins and to cleanse us from all unrighteousness" (I John 1:9). In preaching on forgiveness, Charles Spurgeon proclaimed:

> We are certain that there is forgiveness, because there is a Gospel, and the very essence of the Gospel lies in the proclamation of the pardon of sin.

FORGIVENESS BUILDS THE BODY

The title of this chapter is "A Church That Forgives." However, so far I've barely mentioned how the members of the body interact with each other. The reason is that we need a firm foundation to support the radical notion that we should be forgiving people. That foundation is the character of God, the person of Jesus Christ, and the heart of the Gospel. With all those in place, we can now fully understand that we must be a freely forgiving people.

I've been through two church splits in my life. Both were heart-wrenching. I pray that I will never go through another. There's a saying that hindsight is 20/20. That holds true when it comes to church splits. Many years later I can look back and see fault all around—a good deal of it my own. I could have done much differently that may have saved quite a bit of pain and suffering. One thing I should have done was ask forgiveness for my actions. I could also have been willing to freely and easily forgive if asked. To my shame I did neither.

We, Christ's church, will one day be perfect. When we're all together at the Marriage Supper of the Lamb (Rev 19:6-10) we will have no fault. While we of course will not be divine, God will have made us perfect. It will be easy to not sin. We'll all live in harmony together. Forgiveness will not be an issue because there won't be anything to forgive.

However, for now we still live here. We're not even close to perfect. We're redeemed, but we still have our problems. We all have issues. Because of that, even within the body of Christ, there's still plenty of need for forgiveness.

Despite all our best efforts, we still occasionally sin against one another. This is where we ought to be different from the world. Instead of seeking revenge, we must live as Jesus did and forgive one another. This is the only way joyful body life can exist. We can and must be quick, free, easy, and complete forgivers.

We who enjoy simple church life like to talk about the importance of the *one anothers*. In order for these one anothers to take place, we must be quick to forgive. Paul instructs us, "Be kind to one another, tenderhearted, forgiving one another, as God in Christ forgave you" (Eph 4:32). Similarly, we read in Colossians 3:13, "bearing with one another, if one has a complaint against another, forgiving each other; as the Lord has forgiven you, so you must also forgive."

We all struggle in various areas of life. For some believers, forgiving others is relatively easy. For others it is quite difficult. Regardless, if we the family of God are to be fully functional in living out the Great Commandment (Matt 22:34-40) and the Great Commission (Matt 28:18-20), we must be quick to both forgive and ask for forgiveness.

This is the only way body life can exist in a manner that pleases God.

FORGIVENESS GRABS THE WORLD'S ATTENTION

Forgiveness is other-worldly. From the world's perspective it is odd. It just doesn't fit in with the priorities of this planet.

Because true forgiveness is so rare, when it does happen it causes the world to pay attention. While this will sometimes lead to mocking and scorn, it sometimes gives opportunity for Gospel proclamation.

During Jesus' farewell discourse in John 13–17, our Lord famously says:

A new commandment I give to you, that you love one another: just as I have loved you, you also are to love one another. By this all people will know that you are my disciples, if you have love for one another (John 13:34-35).

Jesus stresses that the world will know we are His disciples by our love for each other. One key way we show love for one another is through a supernaturally-given motivation and willingness to forgive each other freely. It is because the world does not understand it that it will stand out.

We're for a church that forgives. We're for a church that forgives both those inside and outside the church body. We're for a church that forgives completely with no strings attached.

We're for a church that forgives like Stephen:

> And as they were stoning Stephen, he called out, "Lord Jesus, receive my spirit." And falling to his knees he cried out with a loud voice, "Lord, do not hold this sin against them." And when he said this, he fell asleep (Acts 7:59-60).

{8}

A CHURCH THAT IS COMPOSED OF PEACEMAKERS

By Arthur Sido
Unless otherwise indicated, all Scripture references are from the ESV.

Blessed are the peacemakers, for they shall be called sons of God (Matthew 5:9).

The Beatitudes are some of Jesus' most recognizable teachings and oddly are also the cause of some of the most controversial debates in His church. Even non-Christians with only a cursory understanding of the teachings of the Bible recognize many of Jesus' sayings in His extended discourse. Among all of the teachings of Jesus during His earthly ministry, very few can match the sweeping theological depth and breadth found in the Sermon on the Mount. Although Jesus seems to cover a wide range of unrelated topics when the Sermon is read in a superficial manner, a closer examination reveals a number of common themes that run through His teaching here and elsewhere. One theme stands out both for the number of precepts that are linked to it and also for the counter-cultural message it delivers. That theme is the command for His followers to be models of peacemaking.

PEACEMAKING: THE CENTRAL
THEME OF THE GOSPEL

Peacemaking is more than a random ethic of living for Christians. It is at the heart of the Gospel itself. The very essence of the Gospel is Jesus substituting Himself in the place of His sheep and in doing so repairing the sin-broken relationship between creatures and their Creator. This is God Himself in the flesh making unilateral peace with those who by nature are His enemies. Paul presents this truth beautifully in his letter to the Colossians:

> And you, who were dead in your trespasses and the uncircumcision of your flesh, God made alive together with him, having forgiven us all our trespasses, by canceling the record of debt that stood against us with its legal demands. This he set aside, nailing it to the cross (Col 2:13-14).

While this teaching on peacemaking is quite clear and unambiguous in Scripture, the church has struggled from the earliest days with the question of how to apply the teachings on peacemaking and how to model the Gospel of peace to the world. Are the Beatitudes simply Jesus preaching the Law in a pre-cross context? Is Jesus calling on His followers to be politically and socially active in opposing war? Or is there a much broader implication to our post-regeneration lives? If nothing else it certainly is an unpopular notion in the American cultural context. What American doesn't feel something stir in their hearts when Mel Gibson gives his pre-battle speech in *Braveheart*? Or when the American good guys strike down the enemies of freedom in countless patriotic movies? In contrast, talking about peacemaking brings up visions of hippies during the Vietnam War; that is going to get a chilly reception in the largely respectable middle class evangelical church.

WHAT IS PEACEMAKING?

What exactly does it mean to be a "peacemaker"? The Scriptures, taken as a unified whole, give us a far more comprehensive vision of peacemaking that goes beyond "Don't shoot people or beat them up." The vision for the church as a community of peacemakers is nothing less than a living out of the Gospel: loving our enemies; service as the highest calling; humility, love, and self-denial as the most precious attributes; counting others as more important than ourselves. All of these notions run completely counter to our prevailing culture. More often than not the church reflects the "me first" attitude of the culture rather than the "enemy love" attitude of Christ. Setting aside our own safety, preferences, and wants in favor of others is an otherworldly manifestation of the as yet to be culminated rebirth of all things under the direct eternal reign of Christ. Something so supernatural can only result from the regenerating power of the Holy Spirit.

What we find when we endeavor to set aside our cultural prejudices is that peacemaking as a spiritual discipline impacts every aspect of our lives as disciple-making followers of Christ. What is on display in the New Testament are normative behaviors that create a public witness with a foundation in non-coercive love. This love witness is manifested in two central themes. First, we see the theme of non-resistance toward evil, such as turning the other cheek. The second is more difficult to see, manifesting itself in a refusal to engage in coercion through denial of self-interest. This is where the remainder of this chapter will focus.

There are many examples of peacemaking in the New Testament that deal with the principle of non-retaliation. Examples include of course Matthew 5:9, but also Matthew 5:38-41 and Romans 12:16-21. Both of the passages deserve extended study. However, for purposes of peacemaking as a more comprehensive embodiment of the Gospel we initially turn to Paul's first letter to the church in Corinth.

PEACEMAKING IN INTERRELATIONSHIPS AS THE CHURCH

In his letter to a church that has all manner of issues to be addressed, there is one particular passage that speaks very powerfully to the idea of peacemaking in the church. It also reminds us that many of the issues we have in the church today are not new.

> When one of you has a grievance against another, does he dare go to law before the unrighteous instead of the saints? Or do you not know that the saints will judge the world? And if the world is to be judged by you, are you incompetent to try trivial cases? Do you not know that we are to judge angels? How much more, then, matters pertaining to this life! So if you have such cases, why do you lay them before those who have no standing in the church? I say this to your shame. Can it be that there is no one among you wise enough to settle a dispute between the brothers, but brother goes to law against brother, and that before unbelievers? To have lawsuits at all with one another is already a defeat for you. Why not rather suffer wrong? Why not rather be defrauded? But you

yourselves wrong and defraud—even your own brothers! (1 Cor 6:1-8)

Paul is addressing an issue that has clearly become a problem in the church in Corinth, specifically public squabbles in the church that are taken before the pagan civil magistrate. Rather than taking the issue up within the church where both parties would agree to submit to and abide by the decision of a respected leader in the church (presumably an elder), the parties go to the civil courts to seek the judgment of Caesar. Paul's solution is fascinating. First go to the church for a decision, but if that is not available the wronged party should prefer to be defrauded rather than seeking satisfaction before the world. What a strange notion to consider in a society inundated with ads for lawyers who will sue anyone for any reason at any time.

This sort of issue is not unique to Corinth and that era. One need only read the contemporary religious news to see examples of church splits where the two parties sue one another over the disposition of religious property or other examples of seeking a restraining order by a church against a disgruntled former member. As Paul warned so long ago, our eagerness to follow the example of the world in going to court, one believer against another, is damaging to our witness and fatal to the "others over self" community we are called to embody. In our eagerness to see earthly justice done and our rights upheld we are reflective of the pagan norms of the world rather than the enemy loving, self-denying norms of the Kingdom.

PEACEMAKING AS WITNESS

Peacemaking as a reflection of the nature of Christ is not simply a goal in and of itself but serves to make a more powerful impact. The peacemaking nature of the church community ought to serve as a witness to the world, something radically different and perhaps even otherworldly in the face of a world that scratches and claws for any and all advantage. To be a peacemaker within the church is as simple as seeing others as more important than yourself. That is all well and good in theory, but peacemaking is one of the most difficult traits in the church to live out. This is particularly the case in the West where individualism and appeals to "rights" are so deeply entrenched in our thinking. As is always the case the Scriptures give us guidance on this matter.

Several excellent examples exist of how this peacemaking ethic serves as a witness and a model for the church. One is found in 1 Peter and speaks of the way a wife can witness to her unbelieving husband, a common situation in the contemporary church:

> Likewise, wives, be subject to your own husbands, so that even if some do not obey the word, they may be won without a word by the conduct of their wives, when they see your respectful and pure conduct (1 Pet 3:1-2).

We find Peter here advising wives to model the non-coercive nature of the church to influence unbelieving husbands. They aren't called to badger their unbelieving husband into grudgingly "going to church" or to argue them into the Kingdom. They are not slipping Bible tracts in the morning newspaper. Their "respectful and pure conduct" is their witnessing tool, a non-coercive witness in the home. While the Gospel proclaimed requires words, the Gospel modeled does not. Our love and self-denial is a witness to the world, a witness that invites questioning thereby opening the door for the proclamation of the Good News.

IT SHALL NOT BE SO AMONG YOU

Another place we see the non-coercive witness of the church on display is in leadership among the Body of Christ. Peacemaking always runs counter to the ways of the world. Nowhere is this more startling than in the teachings of Christ concerning church leadership. The world seeks the most powerful, the smartest, and the most charismatic among the people to rule over them. In ancient times, might made right and leaders ruled by the sword. Today leaders usually rule with the sound bite. In either case the nature of human leadership is coercive, dominating, and usually backed up with force or the threat of force. Jesus as the only true King models and commands a different way:

> But Jesus called them to him and said, "You know that the rulers of the Gentiles lord it over them, and their great ones exercise authority over them. It shall not be so among you. But whoever would be great among you must be your servant, and whoever would be first among you must be your slave, even as the Son of Man came not to be served but to serve, and to give his life as a ransom for many" (Matt 20:25-28).

Even among God's people the desire for a leader modeled after the world is a powerful impulse. In the Old Testament we see this desire manifested in the disastrous demand of the elders of Israel for an earthly king to rule over them "like all the nations" (1 Sam 8:5). Little changed in the New Testament where some Jews sought to make Jesus their king by force (John 6:15). Even His disciples sought prestige and power only to be rebuked by Jesus. Christ turned worldly notions of greatness on their head and declared that the humble servant is greater than the exalted, emphasized by His powerful declaration "It shall not be so among you". Leadership in the church is the antithesis of worldly leadership. Leaders in the church are to be the humblest of servants who lead through example, gentle persuasion, and service rather than by force and declaration.

This counter-cultural peacemaking way of life is not an easy one. However, when we see suffering, hatred, reviling, and persecution as both normative for the church and a reliable measure of the faithfulness of our witness, our need to have our rights respected becomes far less important. The faithful peacemaking witness of the church is often easier to see where the church is most persecuted. Conversely, it is often most difficult to reflect when the church is comfortable in the surrounding culture. Little wonder that peacemaking is frequently either ignored or turned into a religious social-political mantra.

This Kingdom ethic of peacemaking is not something we can compartmentalize into a narrow set of circumstances where we will allow Jesus to have His say. Instead we are called to model this ethic in those areas where it is the most difficult, turning on its head the world's expectations for behavior. It is just as important, perhaps even more so, to be peacemakers in the workplace, in our mixed families, in our schools, and among our friends than it is to be peacemakers when we are on our best Sunday behavior.

More than our religious traditions or our sermons aimed mostly at existing Christians, the peacemaking manner of life in the church can be one of the most powerful witnesses to the outside world, a critical passport to building relationships with those who need to hear the Gospel. Throughout church history, from the martyrs of the earliest days of the church to the Anabaptist martyrs to missionaries like Jim Elliot, the church has relied on the powerful witness of peacemaking to demonstrate in our deeds the enemy-loving Gospel of Jesus Christ. We desperately need to recover this way of life in the church today. Nothing less than the Great Commission itself is at stake.

{9}

A CHURCH THAT ACCEPTS SUFFERING AS A NORMAL PART OF LIFE

By Eric Carpenter
Unless otherwise indicated, all Scripture references are from the ESV.

I'm not sure God wants us to be happy. I think He wants us to love, and be loved. But we are like children, thinking our toys will make us happy and the whole world is our nursery. Something must drive us out of that nursery and into the lives of others, and that something is suffering. ~C.S. Lewis

It all began in the Garden of Eden. In the first two chapters of Genesis we see perfection. At the conclusion of chapter one, after God creates humans, we are told that His creation is "very good." As chapter two ends, we read of God bringing one man and one woman together in a covenantal relationship. Everything is as it should be.

Then we come to Genesis chapter three. The tone of the writing immediately changes. We meet a serpent (Satan) who is described as "crafty." The serpent asks Eve, "Did God actually say, 'You shall not eat of any tree in the garden'?" You know the rest of the story. Adam and Eve both eat of the Tree of the Knowledge of Good and Evil. Because of this sin God casts them out of the garden forever. Suffering enters the world. It has only multiplied since the fall.

SUFFERING IS PART OF LIVING IN A SIN-SOAKED WORLD

A simple glance around the internet reminds us of the constant suffering that plagues this world. When you click on CNN.com or any other similar site you see news story after story of all sorts of suffering around the globe. As I write this essay Israelis and Palestinians are killing each other over conflicting claims to land in the Middle East. Hundreds of civilians have perished in this most recent conflict. In West Africa the Ebola virus is running rampant. Meanwhile families in Europe and Asia are suffering because of two *Malaysia Airlines* disasters within the last few months (one plane disappeared over the Indian Ocean while another was shot down over the Ukraine).

In the comfortable confines of the United States we don't tend to suffer as much as the rest of the world. However, we still have to face accidents, natural disasters, crime, and incurable diseases. No one is free from suffering. It is just a matter of the details. I do not mean to sound fatalistic. Rather, this is simply the reality of the sin-soaked world in which we reside.

If you live for any length of time, you will suffer.

SUFFERING IS A NORMAL PART OF
LIVING FOR JESUS CHRIST

The people of God have always suffered for living for God (1 Pet 5:10). This extends far beyond the normal suffering that comes from living in a sinful world. Rather, this is the pain and persecution that stems from living for Jesus Christ.

A brief survey of both the Old and New Testaments shows us that those who follow faithfully after God suffer for doing so. The primary O.T. example is Job. Even during the most horrendous suffering, Job responded in this manner, "Naked I came from my mother's womb, and naked shall I return. The Lord gave, and the Lord has taken away; blessed be the name of the Lord" (1:21). Later we're told that Job did not sin despite what he endured.

As we turn to the New Testament we run into Paul's sufferings. Throughout much of the book of Acts we read of Paul facing persecution for the Gospel in one way or another. One incident that amazes me is when Paul was stoned in Lystra. We see that after he recovers, Paul goes back into the city. Later, after visiting Derbe, Paul and his associates actually return to Lystra to strengthen the small church there. Paul's commitment to the good news far surpasses his fear of suffering. Later in the New Testament, in Paul's most autobiographical epistle, we read Paul's own description of his multitude of sufferings (2 Corinthians 11). The apostle does not regret it.

A quick reading of Hebrews 11, the "Faith Hall of Fame," makes it clear that God's followers face regular persecution, some very severe.

The suffering of the saints did not stop at the end of the New Testament. In varying ways and degrees the body of Christ has suffered for the past two thousand years. Polycarp, the Bishop of Smyrna who learned from the apostle John, was martyred at the stake. Just before his execution Polycarp was given the opportunity to curse Christ and be released. Instead the elderly bishop stated, "Eighty and six years have I served him, and He never did me any injury. How then can I blaspheme my King and Savior?"

Christian after Christian after Christian has suffered for Christ. I encourage you to read through *Foxe's Book of Martyrs* to learn about the persecutions of many through church history. Other classics include *To the Golden Shore* (a biography of missionary Adoniram Judson), *Through the Gates of Splendor* (an account of the deaths of missionaries Jim Elliot, Nate Saint, and others in the jungles of Ecuador), and *Tortured for Christ* (a short telling of the sufferings of Richard Wurmbrand in Communist Romania).

Suffering is still happening today. The Islamist group ISIS is today telling Iraqi Christians to convert or die. Visit *Voice of the Martyrs* to learn more about suffering saints around the world (persecution.com).

Sometimes Christians, at least in the comfy West, act surprised that they might have to suffer for Jesus. This surprise shows a lack of understanding that suffering is a normal part of the Christian life. Second Timothy 3:12 says, "Indeed, all who desire to live a godly life in Christ Jesus will be persecuted." The apostle Peter deals with this issue in his second epistle. Peter says, "Beloved, do not be surprised at the fiery trial when it comes upon you to test you, as though something strange were happening to you" (2 Pet 4:12).

We can and must take comfort that God knows what is best for us. In fact, God knows much better than we do that suffering is actually *a gift* to strengthen our faith. In Philippians 1:29 we see this, "For it has been granted to you that for the sake of Christ you should not only believe in Him but also suffer for His sake." The word "granted" carries with it the idea of being given a gift. This might be a gift that we, quite frankly, don't really want most of the time. However, God wills what He wills, and does so for our benefit. Romans 5:3-

5 instructs us that suffering leads to endurance which leads to character which leads to hope.

God draws us closer to Himself through our sufferings for Him.

As Christ's body, we must understand that suffering is a normal part of the Christian life.

SUFFERING IS (SADLY) OFTEN A PART OF CHURCH LIFE

While we may have to suffer for the cause of Christ, God does not intend for us to have to suffer because of His church. Body life relationships should be the one place we find a refuge from the sufferings of the world. If there is one time we should feel safe and welcomed, it is when the body gathers.

You've likely heard the expression that says that the church is the only army that shoots its wounded. While this is a vast over-generalization, it does hold some truth. Many in the church have been hurt deeply by things that have happened within the church. There is no excuse for this. If all in the body are looking out for the good of others and are seeking to faithfully carry out the one anothers, then hurt should never happen.

Many of us who have departed from institutional Christianity have faced a different sort of suffering. This does not compare to the sufferings faced by our brothers and sisters overseas who are actually dying for Christ. It also doesn't compare to the persecution groups such as the Anabaptists faced during the Reformation when they left Roman Catholicism and Protestantism behind (simply put, most Anabaptists were exterminated). Nevertheless, what we have experienced in leaving the institution remains painful. The act of leaving often severs friendships even though no one actually wants this to occur. Leaving also frequently carries at least looks of disapproval if not worse from church authorities. After departing, we often face loneliness and a sort of wandering in the desert as we seek community in Christ.

All believers have likely been hurt by other believers. We've also probably hurt others. This is something that should not happen and should not be normal.

FIVE REASONS FOR HOPE AND JOY IN THE FACE OF SUFFERING

Despite all this suffering we have reason for hope. We even have reason for joy. I'm not suggesting that every moment of every day is going to be joyful. Rather, I'm saying that our lives can and should generally be marked by hope and joy for the following five reasons:

First, God is sovereign.

The God of the universe controls all things. He is omnipotent, omniscient, and omnipresent. No suffering occurs beyond the bounds of His control. As Romans 8:28 tells us, "And we know that for those who love God all things work together for good, for those who are called according to His purpose." Therefore, even our suffering is ultimately for our good. In the case of Job we see Satan approach God. Satan can do nothing apart from God's permission. In Job 1:8, God actually says to Satan, "Have you considered my servant Job?" God grants Satan permission to harm Job. While Satan wants to bring about anguish, God allows it for good. We can trust God because He controls all things and uses suffering to push us toward spiritual maturity.

Second, Jesus Christ suffered more than anyone else ever has.

We do not serve a God who doesn't understand us. Rather, our God has suffered beyond anything we will ever face. In the prophet Isaiah's description of the coming servant's suffering, he writes the following, "As many were astonished at you—his appearance was so marred, beyond human semblance, and his form beyond that of the children of mankind" (52:14). Isaiah continues in chapter 53, hitting the apex of Christ's suffering in verse five, "But he was pierced for our transgressions; he was crushed for our iniquities; upon him was the chastisement that brought us peace, and with his wounds we are healed." Jesus Christ knows what it is to suffer. Interestingly, we read later that Jesus even learned from His sufferings. The author of Hebrews tells us in 5:8, "Although He was a Son, He learned obedience through what He suffered." When we suffer we can trust that not only does God control our circumstances, but He also understands them at an experiential level.

Third, we are blessed when we suffer.

I'll be honest: this one is difficult for me. I don't like to suffer. I live in nice, warm Savannah, Georgia. My house has central air conditioning. We have two cars that run. We can go to the beach basically any time we want. I like my warm fuzzy.

Despite my desires for comfort, the reality is that we are blessed by God when we suffer. This is not the material blessing nonsense preached by the health-wealth-prosperity con-artists. Instead, this is spiritual blessings. At the end of the Beatitudes, Matthew tells us, "Blessed are those who are persecuted for righteousness' sake, for theirs is the Kingdom of Heaven" (5:10). When we face persecution for the righteousness of our lives it provides us with assurance that we are, in fact, part of God's Kingdom. Possibly because Matthew's words may seem difficult to believe, he immediately writes something similar, "Blessed are you when others revile you and persecute you and utter all kinds of evil against you falsely on my account" (5:11). Why should we feel blessed? Matthew tells us in 5:12, "Rejoice and be glad, for your reward is great in heaven, for so they persecuted the prophets who were before you." When we suffer for King Jesus, we can take joy in our heavenly reward.

Fourth, after we suffer we can more effectively comfort others.

We learn much through suffering. This may be suffering from living in a sinful world or suffering for the cause of Christ. Regardless, we learn from it. In 2007 our family was serving as missionaries in part of South Asia. We had given much time and effort to the process. After being on the field for only four months we noticed a lump on the side of our son's neck. It wasn't good. Following a week of not knowing what was going on we finally received a diagnosis of a type of Non-Hodgkin Lymphoma. We had to come home immediately and watch our son suffer through chemotherapy at age eight. We thank God that He eventually healed our son, but that was the end of our overseas missions service. I relate this story because through that ordeal, in which we suffered, we learned how to help others with cancer. I'm reminded of what Paul wrote toward the beginning of his second letter to the Corinthian church, "Blessed be the God and Father of our Lord Jesus Christ, the Father of mercies and God of all comfort, who comforts us in our affliction, so that we may be able to comfort those who are in any affliction, with the comfort with which we ourselves are comforted by God" (1:3-4).

Fifth, eternity with Christ will not be like this.

Although suffering has been a normal part of this world ever since the fall, suffering will not exist in heaven. That is a beautiful thought. It's fairly safe to say that anyone who reads this book will be dead within one hundred years of reading it (probably far fewer than that). After death we will never have to deal with suffering again. Hallelujah! In Romans 8:18 Paul writes, "For I consider that the sufferings of this present time are not worth comparing with the glory that is to be revealed to us." The apostle Peter also understands this, writing, "And after you have suffered a little while, the God of all grace, who has called you to His eternal glory in Christ, will Himself restore, confirm, strengthen, and establish you."

SUFFERING IS TEMPORARY, BUT JOY IS FOREVER

We will suffer from living in this world. No one escapes it. We will also suffer because we carry the name of Christ. Since God loves us and desires our maturation in Him, He will most likely grant us the gift of suffering. We may even suffer because of the church. I hope, for your sake, that this is minimal because it is not part of God's plan.

Brothers and sisters, we do not suffer as the world suffers. We know that God is in complete control and has our best in mind. We also know that we are blessed when we suffer for Him. In the end we can take comfort in knowing that while suffering may be extremely painful, it is also temporary. It is joy in Christ that lasts forever.

So we do not lose heart. Though our outer self is wasting away, our inner self is being renewed day by day. For this light momentary affliction is preparing for us an eternal weight of glory beyond all comparison, as we look not to the things that are seen but to the things that are unseen. For the things that are seen are transient, but the things that are unseen are eternal (2 Cor 4:16-18).

{10}

A CHURCH THAT EXHIBITS PERSONAL HOLINESS AND SELF-CONTROL

By Travis Klassen
Unless otherwise indicated, all Scripture references are from the NLT.

Holiness is pure love.
~Samuel Logan Brengle

For me, the word holiness used to come along with two heavy, overstuffed, can't-take-those-on-the-airplane suitcases full of emotional and spiritual baggage. There was a time when holiness was the name of a list of things I shouldn't do. It was a negative WWJD slogan: What Wouldn't Jesus Do?

A HISTORY OF HOLINESS

I tried to live my life combining what I'd learned from the Bible with the marketing slogan by vehicle manufacturer,

Lexus, "relentless pursuit of perfection." I would read the Bible highlighting a verse here, a verse there, things I'd need to stop doing, and then I would put my head down and push forward, vowing to be better each day.

We used to sing a song by Brian Doerksen about holiness, called *Refiner's Fire*. I remember it to be a beautiful song, and it comes back to me with memories of intimate, worshipful experiences. However, for the most part I remember singing lyrics such as "purify my heart," "cleanse me from within," and "I choose to be holy, set apart for you" and making vows relating to changing my behavior.

I created a detailed personal theology to help me live a holy life, my own personal list of laws, to help set me apart. In other words, I sought to find a way that I could separate myself from the unbelievers. I wanted to set myself apart by not doing the things they were doing, so they could realize I was different.

In my pursuit of perfect holiness, to be a true Christian, I developed a set of beliefs around which words must not be uttered, which food and drink must never be consumed, and which movies must not be seen.

As a male, I also understood my role as a leader in a position of headship over women. As such I would "help" them in their own pursuits of holiness by instructing and informing them of the clothes they must choose to maintain modesty.

Many have attempted to find "freedom in Christ" in this way by following the law. As long as no rule is broken, they remain "free." I created my own set of laws, a better, more detailed list than the silly summarized version Jesus gave. Love God? Great. Love my neighbor? Awesome. But what shouldn't I do?

To me, this isn't really freedom; this is just a less constrictive prison, a self-sentenced incarceration under house arrest. There is the illusion of freedom, but there is still a line that cannot be crossed.

You have died with Christ, and he has set you free from the spiritual powers of this world. So why do you keep on following the rules of the world, such as, "Don't handle! Don't taste! Don't touch!"? Such rules are mere human teachings about things that deteriorate as we use them. These rules may seem wise because they require strong devotion, pious self-denial, and severe bodily discipline. But they provide no help in conquering a person's evil desires (Col 2:20-23).

Some of us have crossed the line. Some of us have thrown out the rulebook, ceased our relentless pursuit, and by doing so, found that He has set us free. Then we found out that being free isn't easy.

FREEDOM FIGHTERS

It's been my experience that the most free among the followers of Jesus will always be critiqued and criticized. Freedom is the envied obsession by all those in captivity - especially by those who've decided it is safer to experience the world through a set of restricting chains. Nobody wants to watch someone dance while their own legs are shackled.

I know, because I used to be a safe Christian. I used to live under house arrest (you would rarely find me outside of my home, my office, or my church). I knew the words that I should and shouldn't say, the things I should and shouldn't do, and the places at which I should and shouldn't be seen.

What made things worse is that I wouldn't let this self-oppressive behavior stop with me. I couldn't be satisfied limiting my own freedoms, but I became intent on limiting and regulating the behavior of everyone around me. Not until much later would I realize how many people I'd chased away because of my judgmental attempts to teach them to be holy.

Self-control is just that: controlling yourself. Regulating yourself. It's living within your own convictions.

A friend of mine once said, "Never let anyone 'should' on you." This has become one of those life-changing little nuggets that has stuck with me for years now.

What happens when we cease the self-righteous pursuit of perfection and let our hearts follow Jesus? I'll tell you what, it's less exhausting.

Another song we used to sing (over and over and over again) was Delirious' "I Found Jesus." A great nineties Christian anthem if there ever was one, it always felt good to sing those words in euphoric celebration, but it always left me with a nagging question. Where was Jesus before "I found" him?

Only on the long journey away from the way I used to understand church, religion, and faith have I truly discovered the redemptive love of Jesus. The holiness that accompanies the acceptance of this unconditional love is all around us. We don't find Jesus. He finds us.

We've been pursuing someone who wasn't hiding. He isn't an elusive Savior who only reaches out His hand to pull you from the fire after you've called out long enough or proven you're worth saving.

Have you ever been to the *Pirates of the Caribbean* attraction at *Disneyland*? There is one scene depicting a woman chasing a pirate with a rolling pin. They are mounted to a turntable, so neither is ever going to catch the other. I've watched them chasing each other since I first went on that ride as a six-year-old. I'm sure they'll be at it for many more years to come.

This is how I often imagine our pursuit of holiness: an endless chase between Him and us. It doesn't matter from one day to the next whether we act holier or sin less; we're never going to catch Him—unless we stop running. Then we discover He hasn't been staying just out of reach as we circle round and round trying to catch Him, but He's been chasing us. When we stop running, when we stop striving for something we couldn't earn even if we tried, we let His love come crashing into us.

FOR THE LOVE OF ALL THAT IS HOLY

Holiness is expressed to us through Jesus Christ. It is not something we do; rather, it is intuitive and intangible. Holiness cannot be achieved; it can only be sensed, tapped into and lived through. We cannot become holy by changing our ways. We've been made holy through the sacrifice of Jesus, once and for all.

Holiness is the heart of God revealed through us anytime our actions exhibit love, joy, peace, patience, kindness, gentleness or self-control.

> For God's will was for us to be made holy by the sacrifice of the body of Jesus Christ, once for all time. For by that one offering he forever made perfect those who are being made holy (Heb 10:10, 14).

No longer am I burdened by a set of restrictions, rules, or laws, but inspired to soar. My thoughts aren't consumed with that which I am not permitted, but with the potential of having the Kingdom of God at hand.

At no other time in my life have I experienced such peace, such wellness, and such wholeness. Limitless opportunity is within my grasp. I stride confidently toward the future, with a spectacular faith that my destiny is mine to create, that the canvas is white, and my brightly colored brushstrokes are inspired by the same Artist who paints the sky.

Humans made holy by a holy God. Not called to be holy, not striving to be holy, but made holy once for all time. Holiness isn't something that can be enforced; it is something we sense, something we're enticed into. Likewise, holiness cannot be earned or otherwise attained; it is the very nature of God made accessible to us through Jesus' ultimate sacrificial act of unconditional love.

HOLINESS IS BASED ON LOVE

It is useless for you to work so hard from early morning until late at night, anxiously working for food to eat; for God gives rest to his loved ones (Ps 127:2).

Imagine with me the love of God. It's a hot, humid day, and you've been working (even toiling?) in a dry, dusty field. Maybe you were bringing in the sheaves or something. Anyway, you stumble towards the shaded edge of the field at high noon, nearly suffering of heat stroke, desperate for something to quench your thirst when through the trees you spy a meandering creek. Your pace quickens, your clothes flying off in a dust cloud just before you plunge into the most refreshing, natural pool.

You stay underwater until your lungs scream for air, and you resurface with a triumphant yell and a huge top-and-bottom-set-of-teeth kind of smile. You drink the cool water, consuming that which surrounds you. This is the holy love of God, filling you inside and surrounding you outside.

This endless love refreshes us and makes us clean. Only as we allow ourselves to grasp the love of God and the redemptive message of Jesus' life can we begin to live and love through the holiness we've been bathed in. There is no way to get more of God's love, there's no way to become holier, just as there is nothing we can do to make the water cooler or more refreshing.

All we can do is jump in.

Section 3

BUILDING THE BODY

{11}

A CHURCH THAT IS UNITED IN CHRIST

By Stephanie Bennett
Unless otherwise indicated, all Scripture references are from the NKJV.

The church of Jesus Christ is completely, utterly, totally unified. Twenty centuries have not changed this truth. In fact, there is no division in Christ's Body. We are one.

These statements may be hard to fathom because of the multitude of divisions that are only too evident in today's Christian landscape, but the unity of the Body of Christ is there—we just have to stretch our eyes out over the horizon and look a little deeper to see it.

Paul tells us clearly, "There is only one body and one Spirit, just as you were called in one hope of your calling; one Lord, one faith, one baptism, one God and Father of all, who is above all, and through all, and in you all" (Eph 4:4-6).

It is up to us to either believe what is written or deny it.

So why the centuries of anger and division, warring over words, broken friendships and destroyed families all over how the church should be conducted?

121

Certainly, there is no one word answer, but part of the reason comes from general misunderstanding about the Word of God as conveyed through Scripture. My own view of Scripture is exceedingly high; I love the Word and take it as from the Lord. It is Truth. Unfortunately, much of what religion calls Truth comes from the treasury of mankind—the artifacts of culture, out of which we confuse what we build, what we observe, with God's Truth. It's a mistake. As history reveals, one era may be certain that there is a devil in their midst as in the case of the Salem witch trials, convicting innocent women of the worst sort of evil. At another time and place the same women may be diagnosed with depression or some other psychological disorder. In yet another era the very same women may be perceived as blessed with theatrical gifts or ability to think outside the proverbial box of religion. Time is a great teacher. Even in our own short little lives we may go back to read a diary from the early years of adulthood and scratch our head at age fifty, saying, "Did I really believe that?"

Sometimes this confusion is more apparent in our individual lives than in the church family, and it starts with the little things. While at the beach last Christmas (we live in Florida) I observed the glittery red nail polish on my friend's toes and thought about how lovely it looked. Then it occurred to me that less than 100 years ago in America there were Christians who saw this display as despicably worldly. We may shake our heads in wonderment or even chuckle over nail polish but then make the same sort of judgments about 21st century Christians with tattoos.

SO MUCH HAS CHANGED. AND NOTHING'S CHANGED

Perhaps to the chagrin of some, these external displays of personality are cause enough for division. For these dear saints it is impossible to think that there could be unity with people who believe and behave so differently. For me, I can't help wondering if the Lord cares one jot or tittle about nail polish.

Consider our more recent history: In the 19th and 20th centuries the church circled our wagons to deride the divorced among us, creating second class citizens. This happened all in the name of holiness and pure doctrine. Divorce is but one example; numerous other sins, behavioral anomalies, and social tragedies have been treated as unforgiveable and used as a wedge to wreak havoc and division in the Body of Christ.

"Well, wait! But the Lord says ..."

Yes, I knew that might be the next thoughts filling your head dear reader, but stop for a moment and consider how easy it is to use that argument with any number of individual opinions or social norms. Examples abound: people smoking cigarettes, chewing tobacco, using expletives, women wearing makeup or wearing bathing suits, folks drinking wine or beer—what is anathema in one era is "allowed" or acceptable in another. In many cases what was considered sin years ago has long since moved into the realm of what is considered normal behavior. And it works in reverse as well. Perhaps the most despicable example of mistaken doctrinal error may be seen in the slaves so many Christians held in their possession in early America. We wince at the misinterpretations and abuses of Scripture when we glance back at our forbearers, but oh, the difficulty we have in seeing the error of our own ways. What is important to note is that we will always have differences of opinion, not only on social or political positions, but on spiritual things. The good news is that agreement is not synonymous with unity.

For example, a husband and wife can be completely unified in their love for their children, yet disagree about the proper tack to take in discipline. Or, the couple can be on opposite poles regarding education or politics, but still maintain a deep love for one another. Surely agreement is convenient—even helpful toward getting along together—but it is not necessary in order to have a fulfilling, happy marriage. Instead, there is something greater than agreeing on all things; it's the commitment husband and wife have made to each other—the promise to be singular in their love for one another.

This same thinking can be applied to unity in the church, and truly must be applied if we are to take the entirety of the Scriptures as valid and true. In many places, but specifically in Paul's letter to the young believers in Ephesus, the apostle writes extensively about the union between husband and wife but then quite deliberately states:

> So husbands ought to love their own wives as their own bodies; he who loves his wife loves himself. For no one ever hated his own flesh, but nourishes and cherishes it, just as the Lord does the church. For we are members of His body, of His flesh and of His bones. 'For this reason a man shall leave his father and mother and be joined to his wife and the two shall become one flesh.' This is a great mystery, but I speak concerning Christ and the church (Eph 5:28-32).

The oneness of the husband and wife is a picture of Christ and His church. Just as husband and wife belong to each other and only have eyes for each other, so the church is the Lord's and we are His. Our connection with *Him* makes us part of the church, not with a set of doctrinal practices. The church is His. We cannot build it, create it, or manufacture it, but we can walk in it with all others who have the same connection. *All* who walk in relationship with the Lord are a part of His Body. It is one Body. There is no other.

If this is so, why does unity seem so elusive? For starters, we human beings tend to be rather petty. If you study the history of division in the church you will see that it arises as much over a partiality to green curtains and oak pews as it does over what it means to be baptized in the Holy Spirit. People divide over petty concerns such as where the nursery furniture should be placed, or what type of pulpit the congregation should purchase.

SEEING EYE-TO-EYE IS NOT THE SAME AS LIKEMINDEDNESS

Another reason we often see more evidence of division instead of unity has to do with the insights we gain from reading the Scriptures. Rich insights from the Lord are powerful. They can transform the way we walk with God, but unfortunately, they can also lead us to think that all others should see things in the same light. It's a very quick jump from there to allowing our insight to become pet positions and points of argumentation. Sometimes these positions become concretized into doctrinal beliefs. When they do, our rich, wonderful insight from the Lord morphs from something helpful and edifying to something divisive. From here we enter the worldwide panorama of over 41,000 Christian denominations and organizations. Instead of thinking of the church as one Body, we begin to think of it as a vast multitude of splintered groups of Christians.[1]

---

[1] As of January, 2011, The Pew Center for Religion and Public Life notes over 41,000 Christian denominations and organizations worldwide. The study was commissioned by the Center for the Study of Global Christianity (CSGC) at Gordon-Conwell Theological Seminary in South Hamilton, Mass. http://www.pewforum.org/files/2011/12/Christianity-fullreport-web.pdf Retrieved January 7, 2014.

When we allow "our insights" into the lead position of our fellowship, what we don't often see is that these insights or beliefs can work against the best of intentions. Instead of allowing the insight to stir our hearts toward greater love for each other we get more deeply entrenched—even invested—in making sure our position is held strong. When what "we see" alienates us from those who don't see the same thing we do, we stop experiencing the fellowship of the King, and the centrality of Christ is hijacked. We start judging, cajoling, persuading or arguing, and instead of mutual edification our lovely insight creates a great rift. If this is left unchecked, spiritual pride ensues.

When this occurs it is devastating. People take sides, and a church split often takes place. Sometimes one group goes on to start a new group or denomination, but mostly folks just walk away, deeply disappointed and hurt because "even in the church love is not enough."

And the Christian church barrels on; its members (usually the most dedicated) settle into a comfortable black and white existence rather than thinking through the implications of our convictions and asking the Lord for discernment. But life in the church is not Pleasantville. We are meant to live in glorious color, the variety of the Body of Christ being similar to the vast numbers of wild flowers or seashells on this planet. The diversity of our God's design plans point to a Creator who loves variety. And, when Christ is seated in His rightful place in the lives of believers, fellowship takes place. That fellowship starts between the Lord and His own, trickling down to include others who are also fellowshipping with Him. I like to think of it as just naturally/supernaturally bubbling over like a fountain. As we all step into the water of life, we experience the refreshment of the King and can refresh others.

Unity is the natural result of this fellowship, but only when the commonality of Christ is allowed to take precedence. This precedence of Christ must be present in conversation as much as it is in the preaching, teaching, or worship—our oneness in Christ is unhindered if we keep that focus.

My observations do not mean that "everything is relative," or that there are no truths upon which we may stand. Certainly, the Truth of Jesus Christ is clearly articulated throughout the Scriptures, but perhaps at no place more explicitly than in Ephesians where Paul explains that our Lord is the centerpiece of our faith.

RELIGION OR RELATIONSHIP

The Christian faith is not, and has never been, a religion that mandates belief in a particular style of worship or type of gathering. Yes, there are normative behaviors such as Sunday morning worship and feeding the poor, but what we do is not the focal practice. Rather the faith finds its root in belief in a Person, One Son of God—the sent One, the only perfect man.

John's narrative explains to us that this One is the way, the truth, and the life (John 14:6). We can look away from this centrality of Christ and occupy ourselves with all manner of religious accoutrement, but without Him we subject ourselves to an existence of getting by rather than true life. Without him we lose our way. Not only does He lead us into all truth; Christ embodies it. He *is* Truth.

But discernment is hard. It takes prayer. It takes patience. But walking in the oneness of the Body is well worthwhile. It is delightful to fellowship with others who are also fellowshipping with the Lord.

This brings me to my final point about unity. Our unity is in the Name of Jesus. It is similar in some ways to the unity we have with our families of origin. Whether we get along or not, they are still our family. We can deny them, but the same blood still runs through our veins. There is a unity in the human family that is simply there, but it may or may not have a thing to do with how close we are.

It is one of the most wonderful things in the world to experience the blessed ties that bind hearts together in Christian love. Many have never experienced this kinship, and for that I grieve. But intimacy is something that is cultivated. It takes time and trust. It is blessed, but this intimacy is not the reason nor is it the ground of the church's unity.

Above all, please do not lose heart. Fellowship is God's idea. It is His gift to us. Don't you think God already knew that there would be a struggle to "come to the unity of the faith"? Paul certainly did. Let's take a look at what he wrote to the Ephesians about the unity of the church.

> ... till we all come to the unity of the faith and of the knowledge of the Son of God, to a perfect man, to the measure of the stature of the fullness of Christ; that we should no longer be children, tossed to and fro and carried about with every wind of doctrine by the trickery of men, in the cunning craftiness of deceitful plotting, but, speaking the truth in love, may grow up in all things into Him who is the head—Christ (Eph 3:13-15).

In this passage Paul was concerned about the cunning craftiness of men. He was concerned that some would draw their attention away from Christ. At the time, among countless other religious aberrations, there were teachers claiming that the grace of God was not enough for salvation. Some were known as the Judaizers—men, who in the very Name of Jesus—were teaching that the rites and ceremonies of the Jews must be followed in order to become a disciple of Jesus Christ. Instead of building up the faith, the Judaizers were actually turning the newly converted away from Christ. Instead of believers "growing up in all things into Him who is the Head—Christ," they were deeply at risk of losing the only ground strong enough to stand upon. Paul's concern was well-placed. In all the centuries since that time there have been those coming in the Name of the Lord to preach a Gospel that focuses on countless aspects of the Truth but is off the mark of Christ. As these congregations are built up around a particular aspect of the Gospel they seem to experience a lessening of the power and presence of the Lord for He is not their focus.

FOCUSING ON OUR LORD

Paul knew the young church could stand sure and steady as long as their focus remained on the Lord. That has not changed.

So what do you see? Do you see with the eyes of the Spirit and acknowledge the unity to which our Father calls us? It's not something we have to work towards; rather it is more like something into which we are called. We have the opportunity to walk in the oneness of Christ or walk in division. Which will it be?

The church that is united is one that is not perfect, but is aligned with the Perfect Man, the Second Adam, the One who has only one Bride He is preparing for that day when all will be revealed.

It would give me great joy to say that the unified church is one that knows her head is Christ, but I cannot say that because we are all on our way. Each of us is being transformed by the glorious grace of our Lord growing from "faith to faith and glory to glory." To withhold entering into fellowship with others because they have yet to attain the fullness of Christ's headship is a sign of carnal thinking.

Rather, the church that is unified is made up of a people who are daily endeavoring to walk in the oneness that is

God's heart for us. It is a people who are dedicated to helping one another walk in such a way that Christ's preeminence in our lives is attained. Are there two of you in accord? Seven? One thousand? Are you walking together endeavoring to put Christ first?

MY OWN EXPERIENCE

After forty years of walking with Him, I wish I could say that every moment of every day I experience His Lordship. I am still a disciple on the way, and with Paul, I must say,

> Not that I have already attained, or am already perfected, but I press on, that I may lay hold of that for which Christ Jesus has also laid hold of me. Brethren, I do not count myself to have apprehended, but one thing I do, forgetting those things which are behind and reaching forward to those things which are ahead, I press toward the goal for the prize of the upward call of God in Christ Jesus (Php 4:12-14).

The condition of the heart is what matters to the Lord, not the color of nail polish, whether we dunk or sprinkle in baptism, or if the communion table offers wafers or hunks of bread. The condition of the heart unites us in one Body in which there is no division.

Friend, will you press toward the prize with me?

{12}

A CHURCH THAT RECOGNIZES EQUAL LAITY WITH CHRIST AS THE ONE AND ONLY HEAD

By Kathleen Ward
Unless otherwise indicated, all Scripture references are from the NIV.

I'd like to invite you on a journey with me. We slip back in time nearly 2000 years, and find ourselves on a dusty street in the Middle East. The ground is hot under our feet, smells of food cooking waft out from doorways of houses we pass, and a warm breeze pushes us forwards. We approach one of the houses. As we draw near and peer through the window, we see a group of people sitting in a circle—women, children, slaves and free men sitting together, sharing in a meal. Wait a moment—a servant sitting next to a master? Eating together at the same table? We haven't seen that in any of the other houses we've passed. We realize this must be a gathering of God's people, an early form of "church". We watch and wait for the "service" to start. It's hard for us to work out who the "pastor" is—people seem to be taking turns leading the meeting. One person reads some Scripture, another sings a spiritual song. One teaches something he has learned recently, and others interact and discuss that topic. One shares a message that God has placed on her heart, and another exclaims how relevant that is to his current situation. One tells of an urgent need, and another finds a practical way to meet it. A child asks a question, and his father patiently answers him, explaining difficult concepts in simple language. The group listens intently to each other, and stops every now and then to pray for one another. The servant is treated with as much respect as the free man. The relationships between the people seem deep and vital, and everyone appears to be engaged and involved. People appear to know each other well and love one another deeply.

We pull back from the window and look at each other wordlessly. We are struck by how different this meeting is from church as we know it. We turn and walk back the way we came, wondering how we could bring some of what we have just learned back with us into our own time.

THE IRONY OF PULPITS AND PEWS

A problem exists with the current system of doing church. The model that gives one person a voice with the rest sitting silently is holding God's church back from its full potential. This became apparent to us when we ministered from the front stage, looking down at rows of people who were used to sitting passively and expecting ministry from the professionals. It didn't matter what we said or did from the front - we weren't able to engage, equip, and empower the people in the pews. The system we used for church positioned us as active ministers, but left everyone else as passive recipients.

The church today has a definite class system. Church (as we know it) is divided neatly into two groups of people - the

132

"leaders" and the "followers." The clergy and the laity. The performers and the audience. The teachers and the students. The 1% and the 99%. Those who "do ministry" and those who don't. It's very easy to tell who is who. The ones up front, on the stage, holding the microphone, doing the talking, on the paid staff, with degrees and titles, sometimes wearing funny clothes - they're the clergy. The ones sitting passively in the pews, unable to contribute, uninvited to participate, their voices unheard, their gifts unused, their spirituals hands tied behind their backs - they're the laity. One group has taken too much responsibility onto themselves (rather than letting Christ lead His church), while the other has abdicated their responsibility altogether.

Somehow the New Testament vision of a community of equals supporting each other, submitting to Christ and to one another, and working together to become mature and united has been discarded. It's been replaced by a two-tier system of status, a hierarchy at odds with Jesus' model and intention for His church. The family-like relational model of mature mentors building others up to maturity has been tossed aside for a classroom/performance-venue model of education and entertainment.

CHRIST THE ONLY HEAD OF HIS CHURCH

There is no support for an elite category of Christians in the New Testament. Paul became frustrated when the Corinthians began to boast of leaders and accord them position and status. "When one says, 'I follow Paul,' and another, 'I follow Apollos,' are you not mere men? What, after all, is Apollos? And what is Paul? Only servants" (1 Cor 3:4-5). Throughout the New Testament, one person alone is given position and rank in His church - Christ Jesus. He is "the head of the body, the church; he is the beginning and the firstborn from among the

dead, so that in everything he might have the supremacy" (Col 1:18). He is "far above all rule and authority, power
and dominion...head over everything for the church, which is
his body" (Eph 1:21-23).

Jesus explicitly warns His disciples not to let anyone else
take His rightful place: "You are not to be called 'Rabbi,' for
you have one Teacher, and you are all brothers. And do not
call anyone on earth 'father,' for you have one Father, and he
is in heaven. Nor are you to be called instructors, for you
have one Instructor, the Messiah" (Matt 23:8-12). Only Jesus
can be our Lord, our Rabbi, our leader, the Head of his body.
These are not positions for any human to fulfil. This is in
stark contrast to the hierarchy-based approach to church
which positions the "Senior Pastor" as the visible head of the
local church, a kind of mediator between God and his people.

A CHURCH OF EQUAL LAITY

The New Testament paints many word-pictures of a church of
equal status and standing in Christ, where there is "neither
Jew nor Gentile, neither slave nor free, nor is there male and
female, for you are all one in Christ Jesus" (Gal 3:26). The
parable of the workers reminds us we all have equal status
and reward for our efforts: "'These who were hired last
worked only one hour,' they said, 'and you have made them
equal to us who have borne the burden of the work and the
heat of the day'" (Matt 20:12). We are portrayed as parts of a
building, none as important as "Christ Jesus himself as the
chief cornerstone. In him the whole building is joined together and rises to become a holy temple in the Lord" (Eph 2:20-
21). We have been adopted as God's children, with Jesus "the
firstborn among many brothers and sisters" (Rom 8:29)—the
only One elevated above the rest of us. The church was never
meant to be divided into leaders and followers, masters and

servants, teachers and leaders, rabbis and disciples - we are all followers, all servants, all learners, all disciples, equals under one head.

The metaphor which most explicitly highlights our relationship with one another is the image of the church as a body. First Corinthians 12 is a well fleshed-out argument against anyone in the church positioning themselves above any other in importance or value. "On the contrary, those parts of the body that seem to be weaker are indispensable, and the parts we think are less honorable we treat with special honor ... God has put the body together, giving greater honor to the parts that lacked it, so that there should be no division in the body, but that its parts should have equal concern for each other" (1 Cor 12:22-25). Ephesians 4, one of the most useful passages for understanding the form and function of church, reinforces that the gifts given to individuals in the church are given by Christ himself, purely for the purpose of equipping "his people for works of service, so that the body of Christ may be built up" (Eph 4:12)—never for building up the individuals themselves.

Paul goes on to reinforce the importance of every individual in this process: "From him the whole body, joined and held together by every supporting ligament, grows and builds itself up in love, *as each part does its work*" (Eph 4:16, emphasis mine). A body where some parts are not able to do their work is weakened, diseased, and handicapped. A church model where less than half the members are actively involved and empowered is literally a paraplegic body.

WORKING TOGETHER AS A BODY

To be functioning at its peak, a body needs every part to be working effectively. Our role as the body of Christ is to equip and build one another up "until we all reach unity in the faith and in the knowledge of the Son of God and become mature, attaining to the whole measure of the fullness of Christ" (Eph 4:13). To this end, those of us who are stronger, more mature or given gifts, ought to use what we have to empower and equip others in their journey. That doesn't make us more important—quite the opposite, it requires an attitude of servanthood. Instead of the "hierarchy" of the world, where people jostle for power, prestige and privilege, we have a "low-rarchy" in the church—in God's kingdom, the way up is down, the first shall be last, and the last shall be first. We follow a King who rode a donkey, who washed His followers' feet, whose coronation was a crucifixion, who laid aside His right to equality with God and took on the form of a servant.

Unlike the power-hungry ways of the world, "leadership" in the church is always framed in terms of servanthood or building others up. We are never to "lord it over" or "exercise authority over" one another as the "rulers of the Gentiles" do (Matt 20:25). The way of love ushers in an entirely new paradigm of inverted hierarchy, where those of us with high status need to step down the ladder to lift up those on the bottom rungs. We go down, not to debase ourselves, but to lift others up. "Whoever wants to become great among you must be your servant, and whoever wants to be first must be your slave—just as the Son of Man did not come to be served, but to serve, and to give his life as a ransom for many" (Matt 20:27-28).

Here is what that looks like in the church: the mature mentor the immature, the elders instruct the younger, the rich share with the poor, those who have gifts equip the others for acts of service, the powerful defend the powerless, and the strong bear with the failings of the weak. Nobody ever positions themselves in Christ's rightful place, as Head of the church.

RETHINKING OUR PARADIGM

Our current structures for church are holding us back from empowering and building up one another. The system positions us either as performers or audience members, as broadcasters or passive listeners. Pulpits and pews separate us into two camps and prevent the mutual ministry and one-anothering described over and over again in Scripture. We need to rethink our meeting spaces, our seating arrangements, our use of music and our information delivery methods to find creative ways to release all of God's people to be active participants in their journey towards unity and spiritual maturity. We need to be willing to step off the stage and into the circle, to talk less and listen more, to use our status to lift others high, and to get out of the way and let God work in his people.

Jesus is the Head of His body, the church.
Let's lay aside our own position,
acknowledge His, and let Him lead.
~ Neil Cole & Phil Helfer

{13}

A CHURCH THAT COUNTS EVERY MEMBER AS A KEY COMPONENT OF THE BODY

By Alice Carpenter
Unless otherwise indicated, all Scripture references are from the ESV.

*For by the grace given to me I say to every-
one among you not to think of himself more
highly than he ought to think, but to think
with sober judgment, each according to the
measure of faith that God has assigned. For as in one body we have many
members, and the members do not all have
the same function, so we, though many, are
one body in Christ, and individually members
one of another. Having gifts that differ according to the grace given to us, let us use
them: if prophecy, in proportion to our
faith; if service, in our serving; the one who
teaches, in his teaching; the one who exhorts,*

in his exhortation; the one who contributes,
in generosity; the one who leads, zeal; the
one who does acts of mercy,
with cheerfulness (Rom 12:3-8).

The human body is a marvelous thing. Made up of an estimated 37 trillion cells, it encompasses eleven systems made up of at least four different types of tissue, which in turn are composed of more than a dozen elements, all working together to function normally. Medical professionals spend years studying the body and learning the intricacies of its functioning, often specializing in just one of its systems in order to care for patients better. Given the body's complexity, it's easy to see why the Holy Spirit inspired Paul to use the human body as his analogy for the church. This over-arching metaphor runs throughout the New Testament, likening the workings of the church and its members to the body, and providing us with a clear conceptual framework for how we are to interact with one another as members of the church.

How does this play out in the church, or rather, how should it play out? How do people of different ages, with distinct personalities, strengths, weaknesses, and abilities work together to achieve unity? Scripture is fairly clear about how this all works.

THE BODY NEEDS THE VARIOUS PARTS

In 1 Corinthians 12, Paul describes the way the Body of Christ functions with its many parts:

> For just as the body is one and has many members, and all the members of the body, though many, are one body, so it is with Christ. For in one Spirit we

were all baptized into one body—Jews or Greeks, slaves or free—and all were made to drink of one Spirit. For the body does not consist of one member but of many.

If the foot should say, "Because I am not a hand, I do not belong to the body," that would not make it any less a part of the body. And if the ear should say, "Because I am not an eye, I do not belong to the body," that would not make it any less a part of the body. If the whole body were an eye, where would be the sense of hearing? If the whole body were an ear, where would be the sense of smell?

But as it is, God arranged the members in the body, each one of them, as he chose. If all were a single member, where would the body be? As it is, there are many parts, yet one body. The eye cannot say to the hand, "I have no need of you," nor again the head to the feet, "I have no need of you." On the contrary, the parts of the body that seem to be weaker are indispensable, and on those parts of the body that we think less honorable we bestow the greater honor, and our unpresentable parts are treated with greater modesty, which our more presentable parts do not require. But God has so composed the body, giving greater honor to the part that lacked it, that there may be no division in the body, but that the members may have the same care for one another. If one member suffers, all suffer together; if one member is honored, all rejoice together.

Now you are the body of Christ and individually members of it. And God has appointed in the church first apostles, second prophets, third teachers, then miracles, then gifts of healing, helping, administrating, and various kinds of tongues. Are all apostles? Are all prophets? Are all teachers? Do all work miracles? Do all possess gifts of healing? Do all speak with tongues? Do all interpret? But earnestly desire the higher gifts. And I will show you a still more excellent way (1 Cor 12:12-31).

Paul's analogy of the eye and ear cannot be made any clearer. God has given each of us gifts and abilities to use to build up the body of Christ, the church. We are each needed, not just in the group with whom we gather on a regular basis, but in the church as a whole. Young adults, older adults, and children all have their functions within the group as we gather. The real key is that we each recognize and be content with the role God has given us within the body, and that we recognize that everybody else is necessary, too. Sometimes we need help discovering our role; at other times we help others discover theirs.

What does this mean, in practical terms? If I am gifted in helping, hospitality, and administration, I shouldn't be trying to teach and be a leader. If my area of ability lies in interpretation and teaching, I shouldn't try to take control of the organizational side of the gathering. I shouldn't expect others to be experts at everything, just as I am not. If I'm a child in the group, I should expect to learn from the elder members, and if I'm an elder, I should accept the responsibility of teaching others either in word or by example.

In a simple church setting, when we truly get to know the other members of the group, it is easy to see where a person's abilities lie, and we can then encourage them to use these gifts to build up the body. We should not ignore people or let them sit idly by while others do everything, as this does not edify anyone. It may take some time to reach, but the end goal is that each person be contributing as God has designed him or her to do.

WHEN ONE PART OF THE BODY HURTS

If one member suffers, all suffer together; if one member is honored, all rejoice together (1 Cor 12:26)

If you have ever had a splinter in the sole of your foot, a pulled back muscle, or a broken bone, you know the truth of this concept. An injury to one part can cause pain throughout your whole body. Likewise, when we get sick with a virus our whole body knows it, and acts to fight it. Our nervous system and our immune system both go on high alert when pain or illness invades.

This is how it should be in the church. When one member is hurting, we should all feel the pain, share the burden and comfort the one who is hurting. When we ignore another's hurt, they suffer alone and feel cut off from the body, and we lose the valuable experience of empathizing with them. We cannot afford to cut off any of our body parts in the church; each member is needed.

THE BODY TAKES CARE OF THE WEAKER PART

I have a friend who had a stroke when she was nine years old. She almost died, spent months in recovery, and was left with some permanent neuromuscular deficits. Specifically, her right arm and hand have no fine-motor control and her right foot is slightly twisted. She was right-handed before the stroke, so she had to re-learn how to do everything left-handed. She still has nerve pain a lot of the time. There are many two-handed tasks that she has to ask for help in doing or has learned to do one-handed. Now in her 40s, she deals with ongoing issues related directly to the stroke. It altered her body forever. She constantly has to compensate for the weaker parts of her body.

You don't have to have survived a stroke to understand this idea. If you have ever sprained an ankle you will remember having to be on crutches, using the healthy foot and your hands and arms to compensate for that weaker part. If your back hurts you may find yourself compensating by using your leg or arm muscles more as you move around or lift things. Our bodies do this naturally in order to allow the injured part to rest and recuperate. If an injury is severe we may have to spend several days in bed just resting and relaxing in order to restore the injured part to health.

In our church gatherings the same concept applies. We should be willing to compensate for our brothers or sisters who are injured in some way emotionally or spiritually, and give them the time to rest, relax, and be restored to health. This requires really knowing the others and being sensitive to their hurts and problems. If we focus only on our own needs we will be blind to the needs of others. We also need to be willing to let others know when we are hurt and need some rest from the responsibilities we have in the body. Rather than pretending we are fine and limping along, we should be humble and reveal our weakness.

Not only should the Body of Christ take care of the weaker members, but the stronger members of the body should teach and train the weaker members so that they can be strengthened and function properly.

Paul again uses the analogy of the body when he describes the self-discipline needed to run the race: "But I discipline my body and keep it under control, lest after preaching to others I myself should be disqualified" (1 Cor 9:27). Athletes train their bodies, strengthening their weaker parts, in order to perform their chosen sport more successfully. Even those of us who aren't athletes should exercise, training our legs, arms, hearts, and minds in order to be fit. As a piano teacher I teach my students to train their fingers, through long hours of practice, to play a particular piece. Just as our bodies can be taught and trained, the members of our church body can, too. Older and more experienced Christians need to be teaching and training the younger and newer believers on a regular basis so that we will all be strengthened. This can happen in a specific group gathering or on an individual basis. We need to be alert for opportunities to train others who are "weaker" than we are, always realizing that the main goals are that the church be edified and God be glorified.

THE BODY SHOULD GROW AND THRIVE

This seems like a no-brainer (pun intended). But many times we find ourselves asking why things don't seem to be going well in our church gatherings. We may wonder what's going on, why we aren't growing spiritually, or why we don't see others becoming stronger Christians. We need to ask ourselves:

- Are we each using the gifts God has given us to function in the role He designed for us?
- Are we sensitive to the needs and hurts of other members of the body?
- Are we helping the weaker or injured members by letting them heal, or by teaching and training them?
- Are we truly considering every member a key component of the body?

Paul gives specific instructions for how to live this out in Colossians 3. First he tells us in verses 5-9 what sins to "put off," and then he tells us in verses 12 and 13 what character traits to "put on." Paul sums it up in verses 14 and 15: "And above all these put on love, which binds everything together in perfect harmony. And let the peace of Christ rule in your hearts, to which indeed you were called *in one body*. And be thankful."

It is only when we truly count each member of our gathering as a key member of the body of Christ that we can function as a whole the way God intended. It is then that we will have a body that thrives and grows with Christ as the Head.

> And he gave the apostles, the prophets, the evangelists, the shepherds and teachers, to equip the saints for the work of ministry, for building up the body of Christ, until we all attain to the unity of the faith and of the knowledge of the Son of God, to mature manhood, to the measure of the stature of the fullness of Christ, so that we may no longer be children, tossed to and fro by the waves and carried about by every wind of doctrine, by human cunning, by craftiness in deceitful schemes. Rather, speaking the truth in love, we are to grow up in every way into him who is the head, into Christ, from whom the whole body, joined and held together by every joint with which it is equipped, when each part is working properly, makes the body grow so that it builds itself up in love (Eph 4:11-16).

{14}

A CHURCH THAT VIEWS
ITSELF AS A PEOPLE

By Brian Swan
Unless otherwise indicated, all Scripture references are from the ERV.

Scripture writers paint a beautiful picture that describes the body of Christ in detail. We read of the people of God, the Bride of Christ, and the family of God. These are all realities, but they also all paint a picture. At its most basic level this picture shows us *a people*.

In the New Testament we see these special people referred to by yet another word: the church.

The Scriptures contain over one hundred references to the word church. After you read, study, and soak up all the verses, I am confident your conclusion will be that the church is actually Christ's people incarnating Christ together (far different from the building that many people call a "church" today). The Bible was written to reveal Christ to us, and that is exactly what the pages of Scripture are doing when describing the church.

During the first century, churches met in homes. This was the standard of the day, where people ministered to one another and grew in community together. In these homes, the church gathered as a people to share in Christ. Special church buildings, an overabundance of programs, and numerous services did not hit the scene until hundreds of years later.

THE LIVING, THRIVING CHURCH

Many Scripture passages provide images describing the church as a living, breathing entity. The church in the Bible is always portrayed as an actual living organism, something that already existed and that man cannot create. For example, 1 Peter 2:5 says, "You also are like living stones, and God is using you to build a spiritual house. You are to serve God in this house as holy priests, offering him spiritual sacrifices that He will accept because of Jesus Christ."

Church is described as a people that others can see, hear, and smell supernaturally when gathered together. Ephesians 1:22-23 tells us, "God put everything under Christ's power and made Him head over everything for the church. The church is Christ's body. It is filled with him. He makes everything complete in every way."

Christ's church is composed of people. These people are very much alive. We do well to view ourselves as what we are—a people. Instead of thinking in terms of static things such as buildings or institutions, we more accurately and beneficially think of Christ's body as a thriving, growing mass of humanity that loves Jesus. Christ created us to primarily need Him for life. However, we also—secondarily—need one another. We live best in community. We do best to think of the church as a living, breathing family in community with each other.

THE CHURCH AND ITS HOLY AROMA

Have you ever run into a group of people where someone's perfume smells nasty, and you cannot tell where the smell is coming from? Or have you sat next to a bunch of people that reek of cologne? If you cannot stand the smell, and the stench makes your head hurt, you may not just be overly-sensitive to bad odors. You may actually suffer from an intolerance of unholy aromas.

Aromas are certainly physical, but they can also be spiritual. Smell perceptions diminish quickly after a person first gets a whiff. Most people tend to notice a smell as soon as they meet with an individual or a group of people; however, the smell becomes less noticeable over time. I'm allergic to these aromas. The smells tend to persist, failing to fade away. In most cases, I perceive the stench getting stronger and stronger to the point where it is unbearable and I need to leave.

This hypersensitivity to unholy aromas is caused by a focus on the holy aroma of Christ. Man-made aromas cause my allergies to flare up, where the unnatural smell emitted makes my eyes water and blurs my vision. People lacking the intolerance of unholy aromas are likely to become passive over time, tolerant of other unholy aromas permeating the air, and unaware of how they are perceived by others. Once someone is no longer sensitive to the smell they are radiating, they fit right in unaware of how others on the outside see, hear, and smell them.

This hypersensitivity comes with certain downfalls. I can no longer function inside certain man-made groups because I can no longer tolerate the smell the system emits. I want to be part of an aroma that is supernatural, of a people whose wonderful fragrance hits others like a ton of bricks. This is an aroma that conveys the fragrance of love as living bricks.

The fragrance I'm describing is the aroma of Christ. Second Corinthians 2:14 is one verse that talks about us as Christ's body being an aroma. Paul writes, "But thanks be to God, who always leads us in victory through Christ. God uses us to spread his knowledge everywhere like a sweet-smelling perfume." It is an astounding thing that we, Christ's people, can live in such a manner that we are able to emit the aroma of Jesus.

This sweet aroma describes what we are to be no matter where we are. In order to get someone else's aroma on you, you must spend considerable time close to that person. A relationship must form that has a common factor (Christ). A person's aroma will not become your own unless you stick close to them. Only then does their aroma meld with yours. This falls in line with loving your neighbor as yourself. If you do that, the aroma of Christ will exude from you and into others around you.

I could not understand what an aroma for Christ meant when I was connected to institutional Christianity. It was not until I was free from the traditions that I could see Jesus and the people that made up the actual body of Christ. When my allergies cleared up, and my eyes stopped watering, I saw Jesus as clear as day. I was free from the man-made induced allergies.

THE CHURCH'S FREEDOM

Freedom has a particular aroma.

Multiple brands of shower gels and shampoos say they smell like wilderness, crisp air, and even freedom. Initially, I thought it was clever marketing aimed at people like me who work in cubicles and want to experience the outdoor feeling during every morning shower. However, as I pondered the words further, curiosity on what "freedom" smells like got the best of me. Can freedom really be bottled up as a fragrance to experience each and every day?

The aroma of freedom smells awesome. The freedom in Christ to act in love is the aroma people smell as we go about our daily lives. However, just being around others is not what matters to Christ. Rather, it is the action people see that gives off the wonderful supernatural aroma of Jesus. Working together is like sweating together, and as we put love into action for others, the sweat of Jesus drips from our brows. This is not a man-made sweat, but a supernatural sweat. It is an aroma others can see, which is an active fragrance that cannot be duplicated by man because God has already established it.

People supernaturally see and smell the aroma when the body of Christ works together. But how can the body and others supernaturally *hear* the aroma of Jesus?

THE CHURCH IS MAKING MUSIC TOGETHER

A trio of bluegrass musicians would visit and play during the time I spent in prison (just to clarify, I volunteered in a prison ministry; I was not convicted. But that does not matter really, because the only difference between the men inside the prison and me is that they got caught). As the trio played, the music sounded so harmonious that it would draw us all close together in unity.

Now, picture a musical Trinity in your head: the Father, the Son, and the Spirit all playing their own instruments. Each musician produces a unique sound. The three play perfectly together. The people of God are a shadow of this reality. We all have instruments we play, but not perfectly. A solo is great to hear every once in a while; however, you hear the beautiful music of the church most clearly when everyone is playing instruments together. We are a people that God has called to play our instruments with our focus on the Maestro—Jesus.

If the musical group (church) plays the song called love, and each person plays to their full potential, the supernatural aroma of Christ can be heard loud and clear. When musicians decide to play on their own without following the Maestro, the sound becomes a man-made noise; others will not see, smell, or hear Christ's lovely aroma. We must follow our Maestro!

Gatherings of people, or assemblies, come in many forms. If Christ is the Head of any of these groups, then people will see, hear, and smell Jesus a mile away. People are assembling as the aroma wherever they are and wherever they go. People are gathering without the dogma of man-made rules. Christ is love, and as His body we are the aroma! That is it, nothing more, nothing less, and nothing else.

Open your eyes, open your ears, and even open your nose. Take the stage on the band platform of life, and faithfully play the instrument you have been given. Know the joy of playing your part in producing the glorious harmony as a people from which Jesus Christ can be seen, heard, and even smelled.

We are for a church that sees itself first and foremost as a people—a people after Christ.

{15}

A CHURCH THAT ASSEMBLES FOR MUTUAL EDIFICATION

By Will Rochow
Unless otherwise indicated, all Scripture references are from the NIV.

It has been said, "There are no bleachers in the Kingdom of God." I have often mused over that. While bleachers have their place in sporting events and the like, if we apply that little quip to a church that gathers for mutual edification, we quickly see that such a church can have no spectators, and therefore, has no need for bleachers.

MUTUAL EDIFICATION: EMPTYING THE BLEACHERS

We believe and recognize that every true Christian is a contributor for the common good of the body of Christ. When the Apostle Paul said, "everyone has" and "all of these must be done for strengthening of the church" (1 Cor 14:26), we believe that he was calling us to give room for each other to use the gifts that God has bestowed upon us. Why is that important? First, it is important because we all belong equally to the body of Christ. Secondly, it's important because that is the way God ordained that His church should be strengthened and built up. Therein lies His plan for the edification of this strange and yet wonderful cooperative that we call the church.

A thousand ways exist for every Christian to use his or her God-given gifts for the building up of the body, that is, for mutual edification. That only a small segment of these gifts are generally used on a typical Sunday morning is not a negative, nor is it an excuse to sit back and passively do nothing. Rather it leads us to see that there is much more to Christian service and mutual edification than only the Sunday morning church service. The best way to see this is to consider how Christ would have His church function during the other six and a half days of the week. If we look at the early church, we see that they gathered together *"every day"* (Acts 2:46). Imagine, a church so interested in each other that they gather together daily.

We certainly do not want to be legalistic about this; we can debate whether or not we can or should do likewise today, or if that was just a one-off of the early believers. The fact is, however, that there are needs all around us. Those needs run twenty-four hours per day, seven days per week. In truth, we would be hard pressed to find a block of time during our week where some brother or sister couldn't use a little edifying. Someone in the body can always benefit from a helping hand, a word of encouragement, a shoulder to cry on, or simply a good old-fashioned hug. It is just as important when two or three are gathered Tuesday afternoon or Friday evening as when we gather Sunday morning.

Edification is a way of life, and not just a way of doing church. It may have its genesis in the local fellowship, and as such it does bless and encourage the local fellowship. However, just as the church doesn't stop breathing after the sermon is over, neither does the church stop its mission when the benediction has been said and it walks out the door. Its pulse continues in the community and with the people whose paths cross hers, regardless of whether or not they also call themselves Christians. Where we sometimes run into trouble is when we look at the church solely as a provider of something for us. While we do personally receive something, it is first and foremost never about what we can get out of it for ourselves, but rather what we can give into it for others.

By way of example, I have the privilege of fellowshipping with some of the most selfless people I have ever met. One brother in our fellowship spends a significant amount of time each week distributing extra food from our local soup kitchen to over thirty families that he believes can use a helping hand. Another brother has repeatedly taken people into his home and offered them free room and board while they try to get themselves back on their feet. Yet another brother has time and again blessed others with free services from his own business, simply because he believed that there was a need. I cannot count how many times that I too have been blessed in my hour of need by these brothers.

What does that do to folks who are a little down because they're struggling with a lack of food or housing? What does that do to brothers or sisters who find that they have begun to sink into a pit of despair because they can no longer imagine a way out of their predicaments? What it does is build them up. It rejuvenates their spirits and restores in them a little faith in humanity. Perhaps more importantly, maybe it begins to restore in them a faith that there is a God who loves them.

It is the proverbial Golden Rule of, "Do unto others as you would have them do unto you." Ultimately, as the old adage says, "What goes around, comes around," because as we seek to uplift others, we too strangely find ourselves uplifted. That is what happens when the church gathers, regardless of where

155

or when that may be. This results in the former religious bleachers standing deserted.

MUTUAL EDIFICATION: THE "ONE ANOTHERS"

The church that gathers for mutual edification does so because it understands that there are a plethora of *one anothers* in the New Testament that cannot be ignored.

The most frequent of these is the command to "love one another" (John 13:34-35; 15:12, 17; Rom 13:8; 1 Thess 4:9; 1 Pet 3:8; 4:8; 1 John 3:11, 23; 4:7, 11, 12; 2 John 5). This includes the related "be devoted to one another in brotherly love" (Rom 12:10), and "serve one another in love" (Gal 5:13).

We are called to "encourage one another" (1 Thess 4:18; 5:11; Heb 3:13; 10:25), and even to "greet one another with a holy kiss" (Rom 16:16; 1 Cor 16:20; 2 Cor 13:12). And then there are a couple of my personal favorites, "accept one another, then just as Christ accepted you" (Rom 15:7), and "submit to one another out of reverence for Christ" (Eph 5:21).

A host of others exist as well, such as "be at peace with one another" (Mark 9:50), "wash one another's feet" (John 13:14), "live in harmony with one another" (Rom 12:16), and "carry each other's burdens" (Gal 6:2). And when we make a mess of things (and who doesn't?), we read, "be patient, bearing with one another in love" (Eph 4:2), and "forgiving each other" (Eph 4:32).

There are also some one anothers that speak directly to many of the problems that we have in the church today—problems which actually hinder mutual edification. We are told to "stop passing judgment on one another" (Rom 14:13), to have "equal concern for each other" (1 Cor 12:25), and we're warned that "if you keep on biting and devouring each other, you will be destroyed by each other" (Gal 5:15).

Such a plenitude of one anothers must cause us to pause for some consideration. How do these one anothers speak to the church gathering? The answer to the question should be obvious; there must be mutual and shared intimacy. How the church treats the "other" indicates how well it edifies, or fails to edify, the body.

We speak of valuing the importance of mutual edification, but we must acknowledge that the church hasn't always done very well with the one anothers. As a result, it hasn't always done very well in the area of mutual edification either. This is not something unique to one group as opposed to another. Failure here isn't only a phenomenon of the institutional church as opposed to the non-institutional variety. It is not a question of Catholic versus Protestant, Evangelical versus Charismatic. The fact is, we've all fallen short (Rom 3:23).

A quick glance through almost any part of church history reveals this truth. Wars have been fought over doctrines, churches have split over relatively insignificant matters, and families have been broken apart simply because religion has been allowed to trump love and unity.

The one anothers are extremely important. Jesus said that whatever we do for even the least, we ultimately do for Him. Conversely, whatever we fail to do for the least, we likewise fail to do for Him (Matt 25:31-46). We err greatly if we take that truth too lightly.

The fact that we're even having this discussion of mutual edification indicates that the church is on the right track. However, I also believe that due to our "poor reflection" (1 Cor 13:12) of the truth of the matter, we are too often still tripping over ourselves.

MUTUAL EDIFICATION: LOSING THE GRAFFITI

Success in achieving mutual edification in the church requires that we strive to get rid of this notion of an "other" all together. Why? Perhaps by focusing on an other we are also inadvertently focusing on the walls that separate us as a body of Christ. Walls do not edify; they only highlight the differences of the graffiti artists and backyard theologians who revel in them. Could it be that, in getting rid of the walls, we end up with a cleaner canvas upon which God can better paint His idea of the church?

I remember years ago as a youngster travelling to Europe with my parents. It was at a time when that icon of the Cold War era, the Berlin Wall, still stood as a testimony of man's inhumanity to man. When we had cleared the crossing into East Berlin at the infamous Checkpoint Charlie, it was like we had stepped back fifty years in time. Thanks to the wall, there was no equality between the German people. Yes, both sides were made up of Germans, but that's about where the similarities ended. Certainly there was no mutual edification. Even if they had wanted to, the wealthier West could do little to bless the poorer East.

When we have walls in the church, or as Paul calls them, "dissensions" and "factions" (Gal 5:20), do we not essentially do the same thing? Yes, there are Christians on both sides, but often that's where the similarities end, and like the Berlin Wall, there is often no mutual edification. It all becomes an us-versus-them mentality in which the other is not edified. So when we speak of belonging to a church that values mutual edification, we have a problem. Yes, we know and affirm all the one anothers of Scripture, but our doctrinal and religious walls, our sinful nature (Gal 5:19), often prevent us from fully experiencing the mutual edification that we preach and yearn for.

But, some will no doubt wonder, are not those doctrinal walls essential for preserving the purity of "sound doctrine" (1 Tim 1:10; 2 Tim 4:3; Titus 1:9, 2:1)? Did not the Apostle Paul caution Timothy to "watch your life and doctrine closely" (1 Tim 4:16)? Will we not open ourselves up to all sorts of false doctrines and false prophets and false teachers if we tear down our walls? Is not such talk dangerous and promoting a spirit of religious ecumenism, and ultimately a watering down of our faith?

While those cautions sound right, and I have preached a few of them myself in the past, I cannot help but wonder if we haven't misinterpreted them to indirectly support our practice of wall-building. Ultimately when walls are erected in the church, is it not a sign that her people haven't fully learned to love as Christ loved?

I especially wonder if this isn't the case when taken together with 1 Corinthians 13, where we're told that all doctrines are simply noise when removed from the call to love. Could it be that the primary sound doctrine that we should be watching out for is being a church that is known for love, regardless of where the other is coming from? Is that not also the example of Jesus, who was often criticized for hanging out with those that the religious elite had turned their backs on? Is that not what Jesus' "Greatest Commandment" (Matt 22:34-40) was all about? When we speak of being a church that believes in mutual edification, we're saying that we're striving to take the same approach with the other that Jesus did; that is, breaking down some of those walls that have historically divided us. Practicing genuine love and relationships with all who call on the name of the Lord, regardless of whatever other baggage they may come with, is our ultimate goal in mutual edification.

For mutual edification to become more than just a religious cliché, we need to recognize that not all Christians are on the same page, both in terms of spiritual maturity and doctrinal agreement. Returning to our previous illustration, the German people today are still quite different despite the fall of the wall. Tearing down our religious walls will not necessarily make everyone identical either, but that is okay. God is not seeking carbon copies; He is simply seeking a united people (John 17:20-23), without which the world will remain unbelievers. A careful reading of Romans 14 should make this evident. We do not have to agree with each other, but the concept of genuinely and unpretentiously loving each other is not optional; it is a commandment. Perhaps that is why the Apostle Paul wrote, "So whatever you believe about these things keep between yourself and God" (Rom 14:22). Could it be that God is less interested in our man-made doctrines than we've previously thought?

Mutual edification is possible with the other who thinks differently than we do. Many of us have experienced this through fellowship with people who once embraced their faith from the other side of our religious walls. It all comes down to learning to see the other in the same way Jesus sees them, as an heir of God and co-heir with Christ (Rom 8:17).

MUTUAL EDIFICATION: PEACE AND HARMONY

The prophet Jeremiah once called the exiles to "seek the peace and prosperity of the city" (Jer 29:7). In our quest for mutual edification in the church, I believe that God calls us to the same today, both in our communities and in the church itself. Edification is all about building; mutual edification is all about working together toward that building. The only way that will happen is when we make peace and harmony a non-negotiable in our fellowship times. When we lose sight of that, we lose sight of the spiritual building, we lose sight of mutual edification, and I believe, we inadvertently give the devil a foothold (Eph 4:27).

160

The church that gathers for mutual edification always has the welfare of the other at the forefront of its mission (Rom 15:2), and it does so only with a gracious tongue (Col 4:6). While it recognizes that it is easy to find the flaws in others and to dwell on them, it also knows that its mandate is to build each other up in love. As such, its energies are not wasted on the perceived flaws and differences in the body, but rather used only on what is constructive (1 Cor 10:23-24).

Finally, when the church practices mutual edification, it is encouraged. And when it is encouraged, it is strengthened. And when it is strengthened, it is built up. And when it is built up, it has the power to endure. And when it has the power to endure, I believe it shall one day hear the "Well Done" (Matt 25:21) from her Lord.

{16}

A CHURCH THAT KNOWS LEADERS ARE THOSE WHO SERVE OTHERS

By Alan Knox
Unless otherwise indicated, all Scripture references are from the author's original translation.

All groups of people need leaders. It just makes sense. Businesses, civic organizations, governments... they all need someone to make decisions and direct others. If the group is large enough, then that leader will need helpers, forming a hierarchy of leadership. The larger the organization, the more hierarchy is needed to ensure that the organization runs efficiently. Again, it just makes sense. But, is this the way that the church is designed to work? Is this the type of leadership among the church in the New Testament?

As with the English terms, the Greek verbs typically translated "lead" and the Greek nouns typically translated "leader" have a range of meanings. Certainly, the terms can point to a person who makes decisions for others, who is in a position of authority, and who directs the affairs of others. However, the terms can also carry meaning closer to the English terms "guide" or "example." In order to understand which meaning the terms "lead" and "leader" have in Scripture, it is necessary to study the terms in context.

WHAT JESUS SAYS ABOUT LEADERS

In the Gospels, Jesus makes a few direct statements related to leadership among His followers. In each passage, Jesus clarifies what it means to lead and what it does not mean to lead among the church.

Matthew 20:20-28 (Mark 10:35-45 and Luke 22:24-27)
In a very familiar passage in the Gospels, two of Jesus' followers (James and John) request to sit at Jesus' left and right hand. They were asking Jesus to give them positions of authority (under Jesus' own authority, of course.) While they were recognizing that Jesus was the supreme leader, they wanted positions of leadership among Jesus' followers.

Jesus' response to the brothers (and to His other followers) is extremely important. In His answer, Jesus admitted that the leaders of the nations directed the affairs of others through this type of hierarchical leadership. However, He said, "It is not to be this way among you." Instead, Jesus turned the concept of hierarchical leadership upside down. He said His greatest followers will be those who serve others. As Luke recorded, Jesus said, "Let the leader among you be the one who serves."

For followers of Jesus, this is a very important statement. Instead of seeking positions of leadership, followers of Jesus should seek to serve others. Instead of following people because of their positions, they should follow the example of those who serve others. Importantly, this is not "servant leadership." Servant leadership still focuses on the act of leading—making decisions or directing others—while serving. However, Jesus focused on service, not leading. He removed the act of leading from the equation completely.

Matthew 23:1-11

In another passage in the Gospels, Jesus warns His disciples and the crowds who gathered around Him about their religious leaders. Primarily, He warns them not to follow the religious leaders' example of doing things just to be seen or recognized as important by people. At one point, Jesus says that these leaders like to be called "Rabbi" or "Teacher." The religious leaders liked their titles and required people to use those titles to acknowledge their positions of leadership.

Jesus said that His followers should not use these same kinds of titles. According to Jesus, leaders among His people are not recognized by their titles, which would point to a certain position. Instead, once again, He said that leaders are those who serve others: "The greatest among you will be your servant."

While the religious leaders direct others because of their positions (which are signified by the titles they used), Jesus said that His followers would not lead in the same way. Instead, they would lead by serving others. In fact, among His followers, the goal was not to lead, but to serve. The question is not, "How can I lead?" The question is, "How can I serve others?"

SUMMARY

In the passages above, Jesus clearly indicates what He means when He uses the verb "lead" and the noun "leader." He does not mean those who direct the affairs of others, those who are in a position of authority, or those who make decisions on behalf of others. Instead, when Jesus used the terms "lead" and "leader" with respect to His followers, He means those who serve others. By serving others, these leaders are an example for others to follow. One who serves is only a leader because someone else follows that person's example and begins serving others also. In that sense, a servant "leads" others by example to be a servant as well.

OTHER NEW TESTAMENT PASSAGES ABOUT LEADERS

While the passages listed above seem to indicate that Jesus defined leaders among His followers as those who serve others, what about other passages in the New Testament? Are there any indications that the authors of the other books and letters in the New Testament follow this same pattern?

In most of the remaining passages that use the verb "lead" or the noun "leader," the author does not specifically indicate what he means by those terms. For example, Paul writes that Jesus' followers should respect those who lead well (1 Thess 5:12-13; 1 Tim 5:17). Similarly, the author of Hebrews instructs his readers to follow (or trust) those who lead them by submitting to them (Heb 13:17). While it could be argued that the phrase "submitting to them" signifies that the leaders hold a position of authority over the readers, elsewhere the same term is used for the relationship between all followers of Jesus (for example, "submitting to one another" in Eph 5:21). In these passages, the authors do not indicate exactly what they mean by the term "leaders."

However, in another passage in Hebrews (Heb 13:7), the author more clearly describes the role of these "leaders." He instructs his readers to remember the leaders, to consider their way of life, and to follow the example of their faith. Again, as with the passages in the Gospels above, the author uses the term "leaders" to refer to those who serve as a guide or an example to others. Importantly, the readers were not instructed to follow those who were in a position of authority over them. Instead, they were instructed to follow their example, that is, to learn from how they live their lives.

THE MEANING OF THE TERMS "LEAD" AND "LEADER"

As indicated above, in the New Testament passages that use the verb translated "lead" or the noun translated "leader" in the context of Jesus' followers, the author is referring to someone who serves as an example or guide by serving others. The authors do not use the terms "lead" or "leader" among the church to refer to someone who has a position of authority, someone who makes decisions for others, or someone who directs the affairs of others. As Jesus said about that form of leadership, "It is not to be this way among you."

How should "leadership" work among Jesus' followers? Those who serve others are also examples to follow. When they serve, they demonstrate what it means to demonstrate the love of God to others. Their example is followed when other people serve as well. The type of service is not as important as the reason for service: to demonstrate the love of God to people in need.

Among the church today, leadership is often viewed as the greatest type of service. Jesus turned this around completely. He demonstrated and taught that service is actually the greatest form of leadership.

What does this mean for us today? If we are recognized as "leaders," then we must ask ourselves who we are serving. If people recognize us as leaders because of our title or because of our position, then we are not the kind of leader that Jesus pointed to. In that case, it would be time for us to start pointing out the servants among us and encouraging others to follow their example.

But, if we are looking for "leaders," then we should ask ourselves what we are looking for. Are we looking for people who are educated, talented speakers, good administrators? Or, are we looking for servants? If we look for servants, then we follow by serving others as well. In Jesus' example, we do not follow a leader by obeying their words; we follow a leader who is serving others by serving others as well.

AN EXAMPLE OF SERVICE AS LEADERSHIP

A few weeks ago, a sister we meet with regularly was very excited. She volunteers in a GED program in our area. Some of the GED students were struggling, and they had asked her if she was willing to tutor them. Not only was she willing, but she gladly served them in this way. As she asked for prayer and help from her brothers and sisters in Christ, others began serving as well. Some began serving by helping with this GED tutoring. Others began serving in different ways as God directed them. But, because of this sister's service, all were encouraged and challenged to serve the people around them in the name of Jesus. In other words, she was leading.

Section 4

IMPACTING THE WORLD

{17}

A CHURCH THAT GIVES LIBERALLY AND GENEROUSLY

By Guy Muse
Unless otherwise indicated, all Scripture references are from the NIV.

When Malachi 3:10 "storehouse tithing" ceases to be the standard for how much and where we give, many believers are left wondering:

- To whom then should I give?
- How much should I give?
- When is the right time to give?

In New Testament simple churches, giving is based upon Jesus' teaching on the subject:

Freely you have received, freely give (Matt 10:8).

Give, and it will be given to you. A good measure, pressed down, shaken together and running over, will be poured into your lap. For with the measure you use, it will be measured to you (Luke 6:38).

This is further clarified by Paul's guiding principles:

I say, he who sows sparingly will also reap sparingly, and he who sows bountifully will also reap bountifully. Each one must do just as he has purposed in his heart, not grudgingly or under compulsion, for God loves a cheerful giver" (2 Cor 9:6-7 NASB).

In order to abide by these principles, I seek to align my giving with what I believe are the three overarching commands Jesus gave to His followers:

1. Love God.

    Jesus replied: "Love the Lord your God with all your heart and with all your soul and with all your mind" (Matt 22:37).

2. Love others.

    Love your neighbor as yourself (Matt 22:39).

3. Make disciples.

    … go and make disciples of all nations … (Matt 28:19).

If I am in doubt about how much to give, to whom I should give, or when, where, and how to give, I ask myself these simple questions: is this a way to express my love for God? Is this a way to love others in Jesus' name? Will this giving help make disciples?

If the answer is yes, I feel free to give.

If the answer is no, I don't.

How Much Should I Give to the Lord?

I find Paul's words liberating in that the amount to be given is whatever is purposed in one's heart.

I respect anyone who by personal conviction believes the whole tithe should be given to their local church. This may well be what they have purposed in their heart and give accordingly with joy. There are certainly many good reasons why a person might choose to give in this way. However, I believe some believers abuse storehouse tithing when they teach one *must* do so, or be in disobedience to "God's Word." Malachi 3:10 is often used as a proof-text where Jews under the Law of Moses are told to:

> Bring the whole tithe into the storehouse, so that there may be food in My house, and test Me now in this...if I will not open for you the windows of heaven and pour out for you a blessing until it overflows.

If we insist on Malachi 3:10 as binding upon New Testament believers, it stands we should follow through and take the "whole tithe" to the temple in Jerusalem. In 70 AD the temple was destroyed. To date it has not been rebuilt. To imply the Malachi passage means we are to now take the "whole tithe" to our local church where we are members seems quite a hermeneutical stretch!

Imagine the Good Samaritan passing by the injured man on his way to Jericho thinking to himself, "... poor guy, wish I could help, but I must honor the Lord by making sure the entirety of my tithe goes to the temple storehouse. This is the one and only place where God has commanded that the tithe be given. As much as I feel for the poor fellow, Scripture is clear my tithe belongs to the Lord. To take from the tithe for this need would be to rob God!"

THE SHIFT TO KINGDOM GIVING

While the last book of the Old Testament (Malachi) is indeed emphatic that Jews were robbing God unless they brought the whole tithe into the temple storehouse, the first four books of the New Testament (Matthew-John) resound with the theme of the Kingdom.

Jesus Himself is introduced in the early chapters of the Gospels as traveling throughout Galilee "preaching the good news of the kingdom." The Kingdom theme is mentioned nine times in just the first six chapters of the opening book of the New Testament. The matter is brought to the forefront with the first command we find Jesus teaching His followers, "Seek first the Kingdom." Jesus came preaching the good news of the Kingdom, not the superiority of the Jerusalem temple system.

Kingdom giving is a natural expression growing out of all that is implied in "seeking first the kingdom." We give joyfully and liberally to Kingdom causes because that is what Jesus said we are to seek out first.

The Kingdom is the broader sphere of Christ's reign on earth right now. While storehouse giving can certainly be in line with Paul's admonition to give what one purposes in his heart (2 Cor 9:7) it should not be seen as the one and only Biblical way of giving. I believe Spirit-led Kingdom giving trumps storehouse tithing.

Why?

Does not 100% of everything belong to the Lord? We followers of Jesus are entrusted stewards assigned to manage Kingdom funds for the King's purposes. The question is not so much what percentage of my money should be given back to the Lord; but rather, what portion of what I have been assigned to manage should be utilized for my personal needs? Jesus' Kingdom is to be first in my giving. I am second.

Could it be all those people and needs the Lord keeps sending my way are His way of letting me know He expects me to be the one to do the helping? Thinking that giving a percentage of my income to my church exempts me from having to deal with all those other unmet needs might be convenient for me; however, this is certainly not what I believe God expects of those He has entrusted with his Kingdom resources!

WHAT PERCENTAGE DOES HE REASONABLY EXPECT?

Jesus never told His disciples what percentage He expected them to give. Rather, Christ said,

> Give, and it will be given to you. A good measure, pressed down, shaken together and running over, will be poured into your lap. For with the measure you use, it will be measured to you (Luke 6:38).

There is no percentage mentioned, only that we will receive back in the same measure that which we give. Some will purpose/measure more than others, but this is something every believer must come to terms with before his/her Lord.

But what about the verse in Matthew 23:23 where Jesus seems to imply that we are to indeed tithe?

> Woe to you, scribes and Pharisees, hypocrites! For you tithe mint and dill and cummin, and have neglected the weightier provisions of the law: justice and mercy and faithfulness; but these are the things you should have done without neglecting the others.

To whom is Jesus addressing these words? Clearly it was to the scribes and Pharisees. This admonition was not directed to His disciples, rather to those still under the Law of Moses. They were under the whole law, including storehouse tithing. After Jesus' death and resurrection we, His disciples, are no longer bound by those same temple laws. Though Jesus was a Jew, born into the teachings of the Law of Moses, He came teaching the Kingdom of God. He taught His followers to seek first the Kingdom of God (Matt 6:33).

If storehouse tithing was an Old Testament command and reference point, in the New Testament we find Paul encouraging new believers, "each one must do just as he has purposed in his heart ..." This is the freedom we have to liberally and generously give as each of us purposes in our hearts.

OUR LOCAL CONTEXT IN ECUADOR

In the house church that meets in our home we purposed to give 100% of what comes in weekly to Kingdom causes. Of the amount collected this past year, it was a joy for all of us together to give toward:

- monthly support for two of our Ecuadorian missionaries serving in Asia
- hospitalization expenses for a pastor's wife
- funeral expenses for a child who died in a sister church
- Philippine Typhoon Relief
- Syrian Refugee Relief Fund
- Enrollment fees for a seminary-bound student
- Christmas presents for children in a poor part of town
- love offering for a sister going through a divorce
- global missions through the Baptist Lottie Moon Christmas Offering

How was the above list of things decided? Throughout the year as needs were made known, we would discuss them during our gathering and together decide what we sensed the Lord leading us to do. Not only is money involved, but in many of the above situations personal time, energy, and effort were given as well in ministering to the needs. Saying that we choose to give 100% of what comes in is in no way implying that everyone else must do the same. It is simply illustrating what can happen when we purpose in our hearts to do something. This leads to liberal, generous, and joyful giving when we see that our gifts of time and money are indeed impacting this lost world.

We teach new disciples to give according to what each purposes in his/her heart. Often we find believers uncomfortable with such an open-ended freedom to give whatever amount is decided in one's heart. In these cases we share 10% is a good starting point.

The majority of the house churches we know about give upwards of 70% to outside Kingdom causes beyond their own local needs as a church. I personally know of many individual believers with whom we work who faithfully give 30% or more of what they receive back to Kingdom causes.

WHAT KINGDOM CAUSES QUALIFY?

When examining the passages in the NT that deal with money and how it was handled in the early church, the list ends up falling into one of the following three broad categories:

1. Advancing apostolic ministry.
2. Helping fellow brothers in time of need (e.g., famine relief).
3. Providing for widows/orphans.

Another way of contextualizing these three is to say that when we give to Kingdom causes we give to events, projects, needs related to:

1. Evangelism/missions, making disciples of the nations.
2. Needs of the saints, both within our fellowship and around the world.
3. Needs of our neighbors in Jesus' Name (often not-yet-believers).

In summary, a church that gives liberally and generously is one that aligns giving with the Great Commandment and the Great Commission. It is a church that understands we give not out of compulsion, but rather what we purpose in our hearts to give. She is a church that gives to Kingdom causes first in accordance with Jesus' teaching that we are to seek first the Kingdom of God. Those Kingdom causes fall under the broad general categories of making disciples, meeting the needs of the saints, and ministering to our neighbors.

{18}

A CHURCH THAT GIVES EVERYDAY AWAY

By Keith Giles
Unless otherwise indicated, all Scripture references are from the NIV.

Let the strong take care of the weak; let the weak respect the strong. Let the rich man minister to the poor man; let the poor man give thanks to God that he gave him one through whom his need might be satisfied.
~Clement of Rome, 1ˢᵗ Century

In the second chapter of Galatians, Paul recounts the time he met with Peter, James, and John in Jerusalem. At that time it was agreed that Paul and Barnabus would be sent out to share the Gospel with the Gentiles. Paul says it was one simple thing that concerned them all, "All they asked was that we should continue to remember the poor..." (Gal 2:10a).

Not only was caring for the poor the one thing they were asked to do, Paul says it was, "the very thing I had been eager to do all along" (Gal 2:10b).

If the earliest Christians—the apostles themselves—felt so strongly about the need to care for the poor as they went out sharing the Gospel, why have we made it such an optional activity in our modern church experience?

Early in 2004, my wife, Wendy, and I were serving on staff at a local church plant in Orange County, California. Little did we know that God was about to bring this verse to life for us in ways we could hardly imagine.

I can remember the first time God spoke to me about what He had in mind. I was part of a small team of volunteers from our church who were passing out "Easter Baskets" at a motel. These were laundry baskets filled with supplies and necessities that families needed to care for their children while on limited incomes. We had just run out of baskets. So, while everyone else on the team ran downstairs to get more, I took the opportunity to look around me.

I saw children's shoes piled outside the door of one room; a welcome mat in front of the room next to that one; a set of wind chimes softly blowing in the breeze outside another door; children playing tag down the hallway from where I was standing. This wasn't just a motel, I realized. This was home for dozens of families on the edge of homelessness.

A few years previous to this I had been out of work for almost a year and a half. We had survived by the grace of God and the exceptional kindness of a few brothers and sisters in Christ. But until this moment I had not known how close we were to the kind of poverty I was seeing in this motel. Families here lived day-to-day on whatever they could scratch together to pay the rent and feed their children.

I'll never forget standing on that second floor balcony and hearing God whisper something to me that nearly stopped my heart. He said, "*If you want this place, I'll give it to you.*"

The kids kept playing in the distance. The sound of muffled conversations echoed from behind closed doors. I stood there for a few moments and considered this offer. Unsure of what He meant exactly, but willing to take the risk all the same, I said, "I'll take it, Lord." And what came next turned our lives upside down in the most amazing way.

JUST LOVE THEM

My first meeting a few weeks later with Pete, the motel's manager, was discouraging. He told me they wanted nothing to do with "Christian stuff" before inviting me to leave. I was crushed.

At home I got on my knees by our bed and asked God for help. "I'm not going to give up this easily, Lord. Either change this manager's heart, or move him out of the way," I prayed.

Over the next few weeks my wife and I, along with two other couples, began to pray together for God to open a door for us at this motel. After a month of praying like this, I tried again.

This time the meeting with the manager was radically different. We talked for almost an hour about basketball and what Phil Jackson should do to help the Lakers win another NBA championship. After we solved that problem, Pete, the motel manager, took a breath and asked me, "So, what exactly were you thinking of doing here?" I explained that we didn't want to preach to anyone or knock on doors and bother people. "We just want to help people with their groceries, give their kids a chance to play on a bounce house once a month, and love them the way Jesus told us to," I said. Pete thought about that a moment and then said, "Sounds great to me!"

I walked out of that meeting shaking my head in disbelief. We were in! And then God started working on changing my heart.

My initial expectations for motel ministry involved starting a weekly church service and eventually transforming every single person there into a born-again Christian. But God had other ideas.

I'll never forget the day. We were cooking hot dogs for the residents in the parking lot of the motel. The bounce house was bobbing up and down, full of laughing children. Our small team of volunteers was praying with a few people on the sidelines. Then it was like God put a spotlight on one specific family and said, "Just love them."

Just this one family? I wondered. What about all the other people here? But since the message was clear we decided to spend extra time with this one family and to love them as God had instructed.

Mike and Pam had two little kids; Mikee and Shanna. They had been living in the motel for several years. As I got to know Mike and Pam I also learned more about the conditions of poverty in Orange County, California. I saw firsthand how difficult it was for those who were poor to get ahead.

One Sunday we invited Mike and Pam and their kids to church with us. Afterwards we invited them over to our house for lunch. That's when God started to soften my heart.

I'll never forget the moment. Mikee was playing with Legos in my boy's bedroom. Suddenly Mikee stopped playing with the blocks and looked around the room, which was just about the size of the motel room where his entire family lived. Mikee said to himself, "This is a house," with a sense of awe. Then he went back to playing with the toys on the floor.

As the realization began to wash over me, I nearly lost it. *This little boy had never been inside a house before.* I could feel my heart expanding inside my chest.

Soon after this, God began to speak to my wife and me about stepping out to plant a new church in Orange County.

We were excited about the possibility. But very soon God would challenge our ideas about church. Soon we realized that He wanted us to start a church that would give away every penny to help the poor in our community.

HOMELESS AND UNEMPLOYED

This radical idea started after we had read a little article by Ray Mayhew called *Embezzlement: The Corporate Sin of American Christianity*. Essentially, the article unveiled for us the amazing way the early church cared for the poor. We read about how they would gladly fast in order to share their own food with a stranger and give up their own beds to allow a stranger to sleep for the night.

As my wife and I marveled over these testimonies of faith and charity, we started to ask ourselves, "What if our new church family shared all of the offering with the poor like this?" The more we considered it, the more we knew that this was exactly what God wanted.

Our hearts began to beat faster as we imagined a church like this. I couldn't wait to get started, actually. But then one evening, as Wendy and I were dreaming about this new church I asked, "How are we going to pull this off?" We both sat there for a second or two, and then Wendy looked at me and said, "We're talking about a house church."

I knew she was right. I searched her eyes for a glimmer of uncertainty, but all I saw reflecting back at me was the same joy I felt in my own heart. "Yeah," I said, taking her hand in mine. "I think you're right." And she was.

We both knew then that God was calling us to start a house church; however, we didn't yet know how to support our family. What followed was a painful process of detaching ourselves from that little church-plant we'd come to love in order to step out into the unknown.

That little "What if?" had started the ball rolling. But the process was challenging, and it was a full year later before I'd find steady employment outside the church. I had no clue at the time that in between our "Yes" to God and our first day of house church we'd have to endure so much pain, uncertainty, and self-doubt.

One of the first things that happened was that we had to move out of our house. The owners of the home we were renting told us we needed to move out so they could sell the house. How were we supposed to start a house church, I wondered, if we didn't have a house?

Weeks went by as we searched for a new house to rent. Soon it came time to move. With no other options, we ended up moving everything we owned into a storage unit.

I was bewildered and confused. "What are you doing, God?" But in hindsight it was all part of His plan.

Our family spent a few weeks sleeping on floors as we continued to search for a new home. I got up every morning and went to work at a temp job to pay bills.

That experience taught us what it was like to be homeless and dependent upon the charity of others and upon our Lord. It was painful, but precious.

Eventually we found the home God had in mind. It was a three bedroom house in Orange with a very large den which was perfect for house church gatherings.

Our little house church started out with just my wife, our two boys, and me. But slowly, over time, God began to send people our way. Eventually we were a few dozen people who were in love with the idea of "being the church" and sharing what we had with others.

That first year our little church was able to give away almost $5,000 to help people in our community. It was astounding to us that we were able to give so much; that excitement grew as the next year we gave almost $7,000.

Soon, we expanded our giving to include people within our own church family who lost jobs or met with unexpected challenges. We never knew how easy it would be to get caught up in the joy of giving and serving one another.

MISSION POSSIBLE

Even though our little church was founded on the idea of giving it all away, we never talk about money. The basket sits at the back of the room and people drop what they can into it whenever possible. Yet people seem to have a natural excitement about giving when they know that every single penny will go to help people in need - often people they know personally. The joy of giving became infectious as we began to connect our offering with tangible results and changed lives.

Our philosophy of giving and sharing comes from Tertullian's *Apology* which reflects the attitudes of the earliest Christians regarding offerings:

> We are a society with a common religious feeling, unity of discipline, a common bond of hope. ... Even if there is a treasury of a sort, it is not made up of money paid in initiation fees, as if religion were a matter of contract. Every man once a month brings some modest contribution—or whatever he wishes, and only if he does wish, and if he can; for nobody is compelled; it is a voluntary offering ... to feed the poor and to bury them, for boys and girls who lack property and parents, and then for slaves grown old ... So we, who are united in mind and soul, have no hesitation about sharing property. All is common

among us—except our wives. At that point we dissolve our partnership.[1]

Over the years, our little house church family, which we called "The Mission," has been able to make a difference in the lives of countless people. Some of what we've been able to give has impacted families at the same motel where God first spoke to me. Some have been homeless, others have been our neighbors, and still others have been next to us on the sofa every Sunday.

I wish I had another chapter to tell you all about these amazing opportunities we've had to touch people's hearts and meet their needs through this practice of sharing. I wish I could go into detail about how giving away everything we receive has impacted the families on our street and in our community. I wish I could show you all the wonderful faces of the people we've been able to touch by simply sharing what God has given us. I can't do that here, but what I hope to do is to inspire you, and to challenge you to consider what would happen if you decided to give away everything in the offering plate and keep nothing for yourselves. What could God do in your community if your church did the same thing we did? Imagine the people you would touch, the lives you could transform, and the difference you could make by simply deciding to spend the offering on those who need it most. Just imagine.

I will say this: for all the lives you would touch and all the difference you might make in taking such a step of faith, no life would have been touched or changed more than your own. That much I can guarantee.

---

[1] Naphtali Lewis, ed., *Roman Civilization Sourcebook II: The Empire* (New York: Harper, 1966), 588.

{19}

A CHURCH THAT
SACRIFICIALLY CARES
FOR THE NEEDY

By Bonar Crump
Unless otherwise indicated, all Scripture references are from the NIV.

*For even the Son of Man did not come to be
served, but to serve, and to give His life as a
ransom for many. ~Jesus Christ, Mark 10:45*

Emotional intelligence (or competency) has become a rare commodity in modern Western civilization. Emotional intelligence means:

1. *Self-awareness.* The ability to recognize and understand personal moods and emotions and drives, as well as their effects on others. Hallmarks of self-awareness include self-confidence, realistic self-assessment, and a self-deprecating sense of humor.
2. *Self-regulation.* The ability to control or redirect disruptive impulses and moods, and the propensity to suspend judgment and to think before acting. Hall-

marks include trustworthiness and integrity, comfort with ambiguity, and openness to change.

3. *Internal motivation.* A passion to work for internal reasons that go beyond external rewards such as money and status. Hallmarks include a strong drive to achieve, optimism even in the face of failure, and organizational commitment.

4. *Empathy.* The ability to understand the emotional makeup of other people. A skill in treating people according to their emotional reactions. Hallmarks include expertise in building and retaining talent, cross-cultural sensitivity, and service to clients and customers.

5. *Social Skills.* Proficiency in managing relationships and building networks, and an ability to find common ground and build rapport. Hallmarks of social skills include effectiveness in leading change, persuasiveness, and expertise building and leading teams.[1]

These are all characteristics of an emotionally intelligent individual; none of them are particularly extraordinary. These are cultured characteristics which can be a sign of someone understanding that the problem is not with emotionality, but with appropriateness of emotion and its expression.

> Anyone can be angry—that is easy. But to be angry with the right person, to the right degree, at the right time, for the right purpose, and in the right way—that is not easy.[2]

I'm afraid that the seats inside our church gatherings are full of emotionally incompetent people. An emotionally in-

---

[1] Daniel Goleman, Emotional Intelligence: *The Groundbreaking Book That Redefines What It Means to Be Smart*, 4th ed. (New York: Bantam Dell, October 2006).

[2] Aristotle, *The Nichomachean Ethics*, in Goleman, *Emotional Intelligence*, xix.

competent person isn't necessarily malevolent or deceitful. More than likely, most are products of families/environments that have never fostered emotional intelligence or ever given it much thought for that matter. This is an important concept because if you give someone who is predisposed to emotional incompetence the Bible they will focus on how the Gospel affects them personally. If you give the Bible to someone who is emotionally intelligent they will tend to focus on how the Gospel affects humanity.

The initial dissimilarity between an emotionally intelligent person accepting Christ and an emotionally incompetent person accepting Christ is vast. The reason this realization is important is that our service to others must come from an emotionally mature place or else it is perceived as hypocritical, phony, and self-serving. Sacrificially caring for the needy and suffering (as the title of this chapter denotes) is the cornerstone of developing emotionally intelligent community and spirituality. There cannot be a more sacrificial provision to the needs of others than when it is to meet the needs of those who are not part of our own tribe. Benevolence and charity is all about *turning the love out* as opposed to meeting our own needs as a community of believers.

> For if you love those who love you, what reward will you get? Are not even the tax collectors doing that? And if you greet only your own people, what are you doing more than others? Do not even the pagans do that? (Matt 5:46-47).

THE WEIGHT OF POSTURE

If we say we are to love the needy, does this mean we are to love both believers and unbelievers?

Maybe the place to begin is to ask what qualifies someone as a "believer"? If we're discussing "belief" then we just went the way of theology and doctrine, denominational disparity, and spiritual categorization. And if we immediately go the way of "belief" before we've even begun then this seems to be a classic case of leading the witness.

Believers and non-believers alike embrace the virtue of helping one's fellow man. Believers (meaning Christians in this context) are not the only root that nourishes humanitarian efforts in the world. Hence, I must argue that if our beliefs are barriers that promote separation instead of restoration then we have taken on the wrong posture from the very start. The posture we have is everything.

> Our posture tells people everything they need to know about how we feel about them. Are they dear to us or are they not?[3]

Some say that care should only go to those who are inside the church. But what does this mean? Typically, it means that only those who attend a particular church gathering should be cared for. But various church gatherings are differentiated by style, décor, vibe, demographics, and racial diversity.

These are all variables. None of these things has any relevance to consistent truth and grace and God's overwhelming love for everyone. These are things that only affect how someone feels, not how he is irrevocably connected to the dirt he walks on, the community he is part of, or the air that he breathes. The style of the gathering is irrelevant! Our posture is everything.

---

[3] MinistryGrid, "Jen Hatmaker: Love Your Neighbor" You Tube. Flash video file. http://www.youtube.com/watch?v=aPIKtKo-spE Accessed November 23, 2013.

Doing church differently is like rearranging chairs on the Titanic. We must realize that slight tweaks, new music, creative lighting, wearing hula shirts, shorts, and flip-flops won't make doing church any more attractive.[4]

Too much time, energy, and thought is put into the brand of belief and style of gathering we choose. These discussions often consume us, fill our shelves with newly penned books, and eventually lead to the general cultural consensus that we, as Christians, are irrelevant because we spend so much of our time on irrelevant subject matter.

UNDERSTANDING THE ME

In Mark 12:28-34, someone once asked Jesus what was the most important of all the commandments. Jesus said,

> Hear, O Israel: The Lord our God, the Lord is one. Love the lord your God with all your heart and with all your soul and with all your mind and with all your strength." The second is this: "Love your neighbor as yourself." There is no commandment greater *than these.*"

Here's the kicker. The person asking Jesus the question agrees with him and elaborates on Jesus' answer by saying that these things are "more important than all burnt offerings and sacrifices."

---

[4] Hugh Halter and Matt Smay, *The Tangible Kingdom: Creating Incarnational Community* (San Francisco: Jossey-Bass, 2008), 130.

> When Jesus saw that he [the other guy] had answered wisely, he said to him, "You are not far from the kingdom of God."

Can you imagine sharing a concept with Jesus and having him chuck you on the shoulder, wink, and respond, "Dude, you totally get it."? I can't. I cannot fathom that anything I believe, express, or perform would ever elicit an "attaboy" from Jesus. Here's why: because I'm screwed up just like everybody else. My tendencies toward self-loathing, self-sabotage, and self-absorption are always flowing right beneath the surface. No matter how well I dress up or perform, ME is still with me everywhere I go. If I truly embrace the concept that I cannot escape ME and believe that I deserve death the same as any other person who has walked the face of this earth then my posture is affected tremendously.

I'm not talking about the tearing of clothes, wearing of sackcloth, and rolling in ashes kind of posture. I'm talking about the daily interactive posture I have that tells people everything they need to know about how I feel about them. I may not get along with the people who live next door to me (true story) because the wife is crazier than an outhouse rat, but I'm not at all certain WHY she is crazy. George Carlin once said,

> Here's all you have to know about men and women: women are crazy, men are stupid. And the main reason women are crazy is that men are stupid.

Maybe the problem with my neighbors is that the husband is stupid which drives the wife crazy. So now I'm confused. The husband seems very normal, benign even. But how could a normal person live with such a lunatic? Doesn't the apparent sane person have to be a little off plumb line in order to live with that kind of madness?

192

The point is that it's easy to observe behavior, but much more difficult to understand why someone is behaving in a specific manner. Causality is always both relevant and rarely comprehensible. It is lazy thinking to levy a knee-jerk assessment and categorize someone based on their outward behavior. And, yet, I've instructed my daughter to never go over into my neighbor's yard, to not engage them in conversation, and pretty much avoid them at all costs. Stop! What is my posture?

My posture might be all wrong. I don't have to willfully expose my daughter to the neighbor's dementia. My eight year old is not equipped for that, but I am. I know how to filter the crazy, reflect compassion in the face of unreasonable criticism, and keep my mouth shut when flames are about to spew forth. Adopting the instructions I have given my daughter as my own personal posture is absurdly detrimental to the fabric of my neighborhood. Maybe it's a constant practice of *me* wearing a suit of Jesus' posture toward messed up people that slowly, but certainly, changes *me*.

> A question that sometimes drives me crazy: am I or are the others crazy? ~Albert Einstein

RIGHTING OUR POSTURE

"We're not called to be successful. We're called to be faithful."[5] To be faithful to the Lord our God means what, exactly? For someone like Alan Graham it means going out into the streets of Austin, TX, and serving those that are chronically homeless. But more than that, it means teaching others (both believer and non-believer) proper posture by providing

---

[5] Alan Graham, "MLF Community First! Village Promotional Video" You Tube. Flash video file. http://www.youtube.com/watch?v=OFzY8 VUn21g (Accessed December23, 2013).

both opportunities to serve the homeless community and physical experiences of personal virtual homelessness that fall far outside of our typical comfort zones. It means learning the essential lesson that broken family is genuinely the number 1 cause of homelessness. It means realizing that without a support system in place there is no one to offer hope and to help pull the homeless up off of the streets. Returning hope to people's lives is an act of faithfulness to the Lord our God and a vital component of righteous posture.

Mobile Loaves and Fishes, based out of Austin, TX, is currently engaged in a project of epic proportions to take the next steps towards restoration of chronically homeless. *Community First!* is a 27 acre master plan community that will house about 200 people with a church, community garden, workshop, and medical facility with dentists, doctors, and therapists. Everything about their model is working towards a holistic approach. This is actually happening right now.

The *Community First!* posture is that the homeless that have been living on the streets for such an awfully long time are you and me. They are not like you and me—they are the images that we see in the mirror but are lacking the support and hope that most of us take for granted. The posture is that these folks are loved by God as broken/beautiful children exactly the same as the rest of us. The posture is one of hope, love, and the washing of feet. The posture is that there is hope only when we listen to God's calling to go out and serve the least of our brothers and sisters. The posture is that we serve God by serving those in need. The posture is to be faithful.

Doing things for other people when there is no hope of a return or benefit to the giver/doer is sacrificial service to God. It can come in a million different flavors, but it is the foundation of what faithfulness to "Love your neighbor as yourself" means. Investment in people means investing in communities and our social problems throughout every corner of our world. Love is the meeting of needs, providing of hope, and "no strings attached" support that always costs more than we think it will at the start. That's why sacrifice is necessary anytime that love is involved. Meeting someone else's needs to the detriment of our own is sacrificial love. And nothing imparts value, honor, and appreciation like sacrificial love. Dare I say that it is a bit of a theme with the cross?

There must be risk taken without hope of reward. There must be investment made without hope of a return. It all defies the idea of "boomerang" love. We never look for it to come back. Are we agreeable with these counter-cultural notions if we know about them right up front? If we're honest we answer the question with, "Sometimes yes and sometimes no." Yes, when we're feeling blessed and the cup runneth over. No, when we're strained and the cup seems dry. Thankfully our God doesn't work that way. Faithfulness is consistent, unwavering, reliable, and always true. It's why the mental image of a plumb line is so important. A plumb line is always true. Any cord weighted at the end when hung from something above the ground will give you a reference point for what is plumb (or straight up and down). It literally never fails. It is faithful.

What if the plumb line of our posture is not our own interpretation of Scripture or the church or theology or doctrine or faithfulness to our principles? What if our posture plumb line is defined by our relationship with the homeless or our sacrifices on behalf of the marginalized or our commitment to eliminate slavery or our relentless pursuit of rescue for beaten/neglected/sexually abused children or the ways we run to the aid of the suicidal or the use of personal resources to mitigate the hopelessness of a single mother? What if it's all of these things at the same time? What if the faithful reference point to a stalwart upward-facing posture is specifically service to those that need it most and, quite possibly, deserve it least?

We are to love our neighbor as we do ourselves. Yet we think more about our Sunday bulletin than we think about the orphan crisis in our world. We believe the church is to be like a city on a hill and a light to the world, but we're more concerned about the new recessed lighting in our lobbies than we are poverty in our city...As believers, we have got to find a way to see poverty and injustice in the world as wrong and worth fighting against. We need our neglect to be exposed. We need to see the indictment of Scripture. And we need to decide to no longer stand for it.[6]

Simply put, these things are an important part of signaling an appropriate posture. Therefore, the importance of our dogma, doctrine, and theology lies only in their value as street signs leading us to sacrificially *care for the needy and suffering both inside and outside the church.* This is our lens. This is our viewfinder to discovering the true heart of God. This is the foundation for all that we believe, profess, and live in accordance to. Sacrificial love, loving posture, and the reprioritizing of actions before opinions is the wearing a suit of Jesus' posture toward messed up people. This slowly, but certainly, changes *me.*

If you want to help people, we have to dive into people, wade into the sea of humanity.
~*Patch Adams*

Compassion a block away looks like condoning, but without compassion we are not imitators of Jesus Christ. ~*Tony Campolo*

---

[6] Brandon Hatmaker, Barefoot Church: *Serving the Least in a Consumer Culture* (Exponential Series) (Grand Rapids: Zondervan, 2011), 327-33.

The ultimate weapon in the face of evil or sorrow, sadness or death, is not stoic virtue and the stiff upper lip but laughter, for where laughter is, God cannot be far away.
~Rev. Peter J. Gomes

All that is necessary for evil to triumph is for good people to do nothing. ~Edmund Burke

{20}

A CHURCH THAT DIES
FOR OTHERS

By Steve Sensenig
Unless otherwise indicated, all Scripture references are from the NASB.

*Have this attitude in yourselves which was
also in Christ Jesus, who ... humbled Himself
... to the point of death ... (Php 2:5-8).*

Perhaps the most difficult thing for many of us to grasp about the Kingdom of God is its complete "upsidedownness." Kingdom principles seem to run completely counter to our human sense of entitlement and privilege.

These are not unfamiliar to most, but consider statements such as these from Scripture:

So the last shall be first, and the first last (Matt 20:16).

For whoever wishes to save his life will lose it; but whoever loses his life for My sake will find it (Matt 16:25).

That which is highly esteemed among men is detestable in the sight of God (Luke 16:15).

It's backwards from what we would expect on the surface. Jesus talked about this "upsidedown-ness" in the context of love, where He stated, "Greater love has no one than this, that one lay down his life for his friends" (John 15:13). And yet, for some reason, it seems that—at least here in the West—we struggle to live out (no pun intended!) this type of love.

In a society and culture where we so often are subconsciously (if not blatantly consciously) driven by a desire for "success" or acceptance, what does it mean to die for others? Is this simply about actually giving up our physical lives in the way Jesus did? Or is there something more to dying for others that should be central to our existence as the church?

It is my opinion that there are many ways that we can die for others, both individually and corporately. I would like to examine some of these ideas with examples from Scripture.

A WORKING DEFINITION

Let's first begin with a working definition of "dying for others." We have a tendency to focus much on the physical event we call "death." When we come to Scripture and see the word "die" or "death," our tendency is to read that event into the passage. But there is more to the concept of dying than just ceasing to live physically.

Dictionary.com offers several definitions for "die," among which is this: "to be no longer subject; become indifferent." This definition comes the closest, I think, to giving us something to work within the context of dying for others. It forces us to ask the question, "To what are we no longer subject?" Or, "To what are we becoming indifferent?" I would submit that in dying for others, we are no longer subject to the self-preservation instinct that so easily drives our decision-making. While "indifferent" might be too strong a word, we cease to be driven by our own desires. And so, with this in mind, I would like to offer the following definition of "dying for others" that will guide the remainder of our discussion in this chapter.

Dying for others means not allowing our own rights, desires, or needs to outweigh the needs of others.

It is, as Paul describes in Philippians 2, thinking of the interests of others, and not just our own. It is not, I would hasten to add, a complete denial of our own interests (this is why I suggested that the word "indifferent" might be too strong in this context). In other words, it is not asceticism. It is not focused on self-denial for its own sake, but it is a proactive seeking to meet the needs of others, even at cost to ourselves (or perhaps without even considering the cost to ourselves). It is not self-denial simply for the purpose of gaining some greater spiritual existence for ourselves; it is self-denial for the purpose of providing a greater spiritual existence (or even just a greater physical existence) for others.

Consider this: Paul does not say, "Do not think of your own interests." He says, "Do not think only of your own interests." We are not to look out only for our own interests, but also (and even more so) for the interests of others. We need to think of others more highly than ourselves. Similarly, Jesus doesn't just say, "Love your neighbor." He says, "Love your neighbor as yourself." So, when we talk about dying for others, there is the need to not focus merely on the dying, but on the life that is brought forth in the process.

In this way, dying for others reflects the literal death for others modeled by Jesus. Dying for others is showing love. It is surrendering something of our own life so that others may gain something in their own life.

CULTURAL DIFFICULTIES IN ADOPTING THIS VIEW

Why is this so foreign to most of us? And why are we (the church) more often seen as those who seek to kill others (metaphorically, although certainly it has even been physical in the past) rather than die for others?

The primary reason for this in our current time in history is that we, as humans, have been conditioned to seek our own rights. Culturally, we have placed a huge emphasis on rights. I'm writing from the perspective of a citizen of the United States of America, whose country was created out of the desire to preserve "our" rights. We fight others to preserve our rights. We sue others in court if we feel like our rights have been violated. We challenge our own government if we feel that it violates our rights. We buy into the belief, with our founding fathers, that all humans are "endowed by their Creator with certain unalienable rights;" and so we begin with that posture of defending our rights.

While it is certainly true that many view military efforts as others dying for our rights, this only serves to muddy the waters further (in my opinion). This is so because it views conquest of "them" (whomever "they" may be, whether it is another country, a dictator, terrorists) as a noble endeavor to preserve the rights of people that we consider part of "us." Even within our own country, Christians are often identified by what they are against, as vocal spokespersons for American Christianity crying loudly about their rights being taken away and adopting a language of warfare in their rhetoric.

But what would a church look like (I'm speaking of the universal church, not a particular organization) that did not focus on its own rights, but rather looked out for the interests of others?

LIVING FOR OTHERS

Perhaps it would be helpful if we re-phrased the concept of "dying for others" into "living for others." What would this look like?

Picture a community where everyone's needs are taken care of. No one has need of anything because they share all things in common. Meals are enjoyed together, and all have plenty to eat. And the best part is that the world around them knows them for their love - a selfless, giving love.

Sound utopian? Too idealistic? This was the community of believers shortly after Jesus ascended and the Holy Spirit had come upon them. This was something that was quite obviously noticeable outside their community because the text tells us that they had, "favor with all the people."

"All those who had believed were together and had all things in common; and they began selling their property and possessions and were sharing them with all, as anyone might have need. Day by day continuing with one mind in the temple, and breaking bread from house to house, they were taking their meals together with gladness and sincerity of heart, praising God and having favor with all the people" (Acts 2:44-47a).

How have we come so far from what that community stood for? How have we become a body known more for what we are against? How have we gotten to the point where we are more concerned about our own rights and protections? And this is not a problem just with how we treat people outside the church, but even within the church itself.

It would be amazing to see the church become known for its love, especially sacrificial love, as the church embraces its call to die for others. It would be an incredible testimony to the very fact that Jesus gave up His life for others.

Unfortunately, many often mistake dying for others as weakness. In our age of increasingly acceptable violence, the notion of actually giving up our lives in any way for others is viewed disparagingly as an undesirable characteristic. It's not that looking out for the needs of others is weakness. It is, indeed, a greater strength.

I have seen a particular quote attributed to various sources, so I am unsure of its origin. But it simply says, "A strong man stands up for himself, a stronger man stands up for others." This underscores the truth that looking out for others is not a sign of weakness. If I could rephrase that quote, I would say a strong man stands up for himself, a stronger man gives himself up for others. Or, as James M. Barrie put it, "The best place a person can die is where they die for others."

CONCLUSION

Recently, I had the opportunity to view the 2013 Disney movie *Frozen*. Much of the movie seemed like rather standard Disney fare. When the plot called for "an act of true love," the assumption (even spoken by some of the characters) is that the heroine needed to kiss the man to whom she was engaged to be married. (Spoiler alert!) But I was completely stunned and moved when it turned out that the "act of true love" was actually her giving her life to save her sister. As I realized that, for once, Disney got the truth of the Gospel, I couldn't hold back my reaction. Knowing that I was in the process of writing this chapter on this very topic, I immediately made the connection. As Olaf said in that movie, "Love is putting someone else's needs before yours." And true love is being willing to do that, even to the point of death.

I conclude with this reminder from 1 Corinthians 13: "And if I give all my possessions to feed the poor, and if I surrender my body to be burned, but do not have love, it profits me nothing." Let us not merely die for others for the sake of dying, but to show our love to those around us who desperately need to see it.

{21}

A CHURCH THAT SEEKS JUSTICE

By J. Michael Jones
Unless otherwise indicated, all Scripture references are from the NIV.

*In my early evangelical days, justice to me
was punitive, coming from a mighty and
righteous God ... Now I see justice as a protective justice, defending the innocent, lifting
up the helpless, and making wrongs right ...*

Justice has always been in the lexicon of my Christian ide-
als. This was the case as I grew up as a Southern Baptist in
the 1960s and through my evangelical years of the seventies
and eighties. The concept even survived my 1990's decade of
personal mayhem where I was rummaging for answers and
meaning; I examined every page of Scripture and analyzed
books of church history, philosophy, and theology (this following in the wake of a catastrophic missionary experience).
Justice emerged on this side of my personal reformation not

only as a more prominent concept, but also having been redefined in its Biblical and philosophical aspects.

The fact that justice has become so significant in the narrative of my Christian faith is illustrated by one of my life verses. Micah 6:8 says, "He has shown you, O mortal, what is good. And what does the Lord require of you? To act justly and to love mercy and to walk humbly with your God." This passage has led to practical manifestations in my life. For example, in 2005 I found myself living in a pup tent in northwest Pakistan near the epicenter of a major earthquake. In 2009 I walked eighty miles over the Himalayas to see patients in a stone school near the border of Tibet. Additionally, my new notion of justice led me to a career of working with patients in chronic pain here in the U.S. (this in lieu of my original intent of sharing the Gospel among Muslims in their homeland). But I must first discuss the boundaries of this justice and bring the heart of its meaning into clearer focus. The best place to start is to compare my new understanding of justice to my old one like a transparency overlay.

A PUNITIVE JUSTICE

To speak in simple terms, I believe that in my early evangelical days, justice to me was punitive, coming from a mighty and righteous God. In the seventies we believed we were living in the last days. Soon Jesus was going to return on a white horse to bring judgment, and that judgment was God's justice. In my deep places, almost at a subconscious level, I wanted God to vindicate us evangelicals by striking down those who had mocked us, either by their direct words, by their actions of not believing in what we believed in, or by openly celebrating their sin.

A PROTECTIVE JUSTICE

Now I see justice as a protective justice, defending the innocent, lifting up the helpless, and making wrongs right as expressed in Psalm 140:12, "I know that the Lord secures justice for the poor and upholds the cause of the needy." This change that occurred in my perspective wasn't a simple eureka moment when verses like this one suddenly soaked in and made sense. Before my decade of transformation, those verses acted like drops of water beading up on a well-waxed rain coat. It took a fundamental shift in my understanding of creation and the nature of mankind before these words of Scripture became penetrable.

THE METAPHYSICAL BASIS OF JUSTICE

The area of my personal tension was related to the much grander conflict that Christianity has grappled with since the manger: the metaphysical question of what is the proper relationship between the material and unseen. Rather than a concept of God creating perfectly in two distinct but equal realms, the Greeks (under a Platonic influence) viewed the two realms of reality as hierarchical with the spiritual being above and superior to the material. It was within this incubator that the early church began to take shape. I believe this tension alone was responsible for most, if not all, of the church's conflicts—including the thirteen or so views lumped together under the title of "Early Christian Heresies." If you examine each one, you will see that residing in the core of each issue is the proper relationship of Jesus with the rest of the spiritual deity. It came down to a metaphysical conflict: If Jesus was material then He couldn't have been divine, and if divine, then not material.

The way that this hypothetical question relates to justice has to do with the state of creation. In my early Christian days I subscribed to the more dualistic view that creation, by the very fact it was material, was inherently inferior if not blatantly evil. While I may have blamed this on the fall, even without the fall, creation—being material—felt dirty or what we called "worldly." Within that context justice can only mean a punitive justice. If we are all created in a disgusting state, more so if we are fallen, then we all deserve punishment ... and little else. God comes to either punish—or at best—to look the other way if we are under the blood of Christ.

In my new perspective, I see creation not as inferior to the spiritual realm but wonderful, intrinsically magnificent ... simply because it is God's stuff. For example in Genesis 1:10 it says, "God called the dry ground 'land,' and the gathered waters he called 'seas.' And God saw that it was good." God didn't say, "I messed up and made a bunch of lousy crap."

If this applies to nature, it applies to all of humanity. If God made us in a wonderful state, being reflective of his very character (even if that state is contaminated by the fall of Adam), all men and women and the entire material universe are still glorious. Because we are begotten of God, and this must be in a passive voice, we are deserving.

A DESERVING JUSTICE

This sounded a bit creepy to me at first, using terms like "deserve." I felt like I was being arrogant, seeking a prosperity Gospel or maybe aligning myself with humanists. But our deserving is intrinsic, universal and, contained. What I mean by "contained" is that we do not possess unlimited deserving that could quickly deteriorate into the mollycoddling of prosperity. When I was in college I was quite involved with a parachurch organization which owned a large conference center. We students would compete for positions to volunteer at this resort for the summer as it was considered discipleship training. It was very hard work. One summer a friend was given a position as a trainee at this resort. After working all day he was tired and came out to the office to ask the staff man if he could take a rest. His choice of words was most unfortunate, and I honestly believe it was due to a subliminal influence from a popular *McDonald's* commercial. He said, "I've been setting up for the meeting for over eight hours and I think I deserve a break now."

The staff man took off his glasses, laid them on his desk, stood up, and looked at the young man with a soft smile. "Son," he said, "What you deserve is to burn in the tortuous fires of hell for all eternity ... everything beyond that is a blessing."

My friend went back to work feeling horrible and never asked for a break again. I felt "blessed" that I hadn't been the one to have said such a thing. But this was the way we thought. How could justice have meaning for despicable, undeserving people such as us?

When you look at the material world and the people created out of the material dust, by the perfect creative power of the infinite God, you must understand that they deserve justice. Justice is fairness. It is not wealth or pandering. It is a child who deserves two loving parents and food to sustain him. It is a young woman who deserves to be respected and honored by men. It is a society that deserves to live in peace and to go to the market in safety, without being shot at. It is the young mother who deserves to see her kids grow up and not killed in some thoughtless accident. It is man who deserves freedom from incarceration if he has violated no laws. It is the farmer in rural Africa, toiling under the hot sun day after day, who deserves not to be exploited by conmen or robbed by thieves. It is 500 young girls sitting in their stone school in Balakot, Pakistan studying Urdu grammar who deserve to learn in peace and giggles of happiness. This, rather than the mountain falling in on them, crushing them to death in a second's notice. I heard some Muslims in Pakistan say it was a punitive justice, Allah striking down girls for going to school. I heard evangelicals in America imply it was God's punishment on the 87,000 killed by the earthquake, retribution for the terrorist attacks on 9-11.

True, protective justice, is the young mother of three little boys deserving to see them grow up, rather than her succumbing to breast cancer at age 32. It is the Palestinian family that deserves the same respect, the same political rights as the Jewish family across the fence. It is the man deserving to live his life out in good health instead of being tormented by severe pain for forty years. This is the justice I believe in.

God created us and this material world in glory. By resisting these injustices, we are honoring God's original intent. Accepting injustices as God's punishment is a great misunderstanding of God and the universe He has made. Once I understood this connotation of justice, verses like Jeremiah 9:24 made perfect sense:

"... but let the one who boasts boast about this: that they have the understanding to know me, that I am the Lord, who exercises kindness, justice and righteousness on earth, for in these I delight," declares the Lord.

Other verses state similar truths:

The righteous care about justice for the poor, but the wicked have no such concern (Prov 29:7).

Learn to do right; seek justice. Defend the oppressed. Take up the cause of the fatherless; plead the case of the widow (Isa 1:17).

Woe to those who make unjust laws, to those who issue oppressive decrees, to deprive the poor of their rights and withhold justice from the oppressed of my people, making widows their prey and robbing the fatherless (Isa 10:1-2).

God's overwhelming concern about justice is not limited to the Old Testament. New Testament passages such as Matthew 23:23 illustrate God's devotion to this principle:

Woe to you, teachers of the law and Pharisees, you hypocrites! You give a tenth of your spices—mint, dill and cumin. But you have neglected the more important matters of the law—justice, mercy and faithfulness. You should have practiced the latter, without neglecting the former.

A JUSTICE BASED IN CREATION

Humans are separated from the rest of creation by the fact that we are created in God's personal image. Because of this our justice supersedes, but does not nullify, the justice of the rest of creation. Because all of creation is begotten from God, through His creative act, all of creation deserves God's justice.

The first time I stood in front of the *Mona Lisa*—well protected behind bullet-proof glass and guards nearby—I was surprised by the simplicity of the painting. I believe any skilled artist, such as my sister, could reproduce it rather well. But what makes it the most famous, and probably the most valuable piece of art in the world, is its history and the fact that it was created by Leonardo De Vinci. This is a dim reflection of how the value of creation is intertwined with the value of the creator. We humans hold an even more special place in the creative work of the artist as His only self-portrait.

This intrinsic value is very different from the pantheists who see creation as valuable, not because it was created by God, but because it is god. This is a vital point that I must be clear about. In the Christian perspective, creation is outside of God, by His deliberate act. Therefore, it is inferior to Him but not diabolically opposite as the word "worldly" might imply in some settings.

AN ALL-ENCOMPASSING JUSTICE

The Christian justice I believe in can also take on the practical meaning that no animal within the animal kingdom deserves cruelty, but instead, deserves good food, kindness, freedom and love. Much of the animal rights movement of today has flown out of the humanist watershed rather than the Christian one. It was not that long ago that the Christian paradigm even gave permission to animal cruelty because animals were seen as disgusting beasts of this inferior and evil, material world. As the Puritan William Bradford described the new world, "Besides, what could they see but a hideous and desolate wilderness, full of wild beasts and wild men— and what multiples there might be of them they know not" (from William Bradford's *Of Plymouth Plantation*, 1651).

The same can be said for inanimate creation. It too is by God's design and creative efforts. Although while not perfect due to the fall of Adam, it is still glorious, and it too deserves justice. This form of justice demands that the planet be treated with ecological respect. As recent as my Christian experience in the seventies we were known to throw our trash in the woods and laugh because we, as Christians, knew that this worthless earth was about to be totally destroyed by God. We thought that God viewed the planet like a burnt and ruined lasagna.

SUMMARY

In summary, as a Christian I believe it is our primary responsibility to bring justice to people ... all people. It doesn't matter the color of their skin, the fullness of their bank accounts, the language they speak, their state of mental health, their sexual orientation, their religion, and even whether or not they have committed horrible crimes. Simply because they were created by God, and because of that alone, they have an infinite and intrinsic value and deserve justice.

{22}

A CHURCH THAT RESTORES DIGNITY WHERE IT'S BEEN LOST

By Kathy Escobar
Unless otherwise indicated, all Scripture references are from the NLT.

When I first met Sherrie she wouldn't look me in the eye. Skittish, scared, and filled with shame, she took a big risk and contacted The Refuge, our faith community, to ask for some help to get out of an abusive relationship. Our first meeting was rough. Tears and a painful story spilled out, and I discovered she was yet another woman in this town who had been beaten down and was desperate for some hope.

When I first met James, he was sitting in the corner of the room with his head hung low, clearly not wanting to talk to anyone. Anxious, skeptical, and filled with pain, the last place he wanted to be was in church at a recovery meeting. But his advocate had told him it was worth trying so he showed up despite his hesitations. We talked for a few minutes at the end of the evening, and I could feel a little bit of warmth seep into our conversation. However, I knew it might be years before the shell he had built around his heart to protect himself for so many years might crack open.

I know a lot of people like Sherrie and James. Some are rich, and some are poor. Some are educated and others have never graduated from high school. Some have kids while others don't. Some are married, and others never have. Some are leaders, and others are followers. Some call Jesus their God while others lost their faith a long time ago. Their circumstances might be different but their stories are the same. The thread that binds them together is that life circumstances and relationships have somehow stripped them of their worth, dignity, and voice.

They've been devalued, silenced, used, controlled, diminished to the point where their dignity as God's precious children, created in His image, has been lost. It's been buried underneath the rubble of real life.

Shame, brokenness, control, loneliness, addictions, depression, illness, poverty, oppression, bad theology, and a host of other human afflictions often bury our dignity. It's not gone. Nothing can ever separate us from God's love and His image imprinted on every fabric of our being. This image is our basic dignity, value, and worth. It is the one thing we all have in common. When the fall of mankind happened in Genesis 3 this image was not extinguished, but we are all aware of our humanity and the brokenness that can often bury our dignity.

HOW CAN DIGNITY BE RESTORED?

We all know the answer is "Jesus!" I believe that is true, and it makes me think of Psalm 3:3 which says, "But you, LORD, are a shield around me, my glory, the One who lifts my head high." Over and over in the Gospels we see Jesus restoring dignity where it had been lost, touching lepers, healing the sick, and advocating for the marginalized. Yes, Jesus does lift our heads. He is the ultimate dignity restorer, the One who heals our wounds and restores us to our rightful place as God's beloved. But the reality for folks like James and Sherrie and many others I know is that the likelihood of them experiencing an encounter with Jesus out of the clear blue sky is slim to none.

It's why Jesus called us to be His hands and feet, vessels of His love.

And it's the work of the church—to call out the dignity in each other that has been buried underneath the rubble.

The reality for many people like James and Sherrie is that they have intersected with people claiming the name of Jesus who have added to the rubble. They've often been shamed. They've been rejected. They've been told that they "just need to work harder, try harder, pray harder." They have been on the margins of every group they've ever been in. They've never had anyone to encourage them in their gifts or help them believe that they were worth something. They've never known what it feels like to be loved, honored, cherished, and respected. They've never been in a place where their dignity could actually be restored in a tangible way that they felt and experienced.

WORDS AREN'T ENOUGH

Telling Sherrie and James that they matter to God won't make a lasting difference. I've learned that words mean little when it comes to healing these deep and painful life wounds. What makes the biggest difference is actually seeing and experiencing something different.

This is why the church is such an important gift to the world. The body of Christ is meant to be a healing agent in restoring dignity. It's the place to clear the rubble together.

The other day I was with a friend from The Refuge who is healing from abuse from her past; it's a hard road and some days are better than others. She "knows" all the right words about God loving and protecting her; she was a youth leader for years. But the right words don't heal the deep wounds in her heart that she felt she couldn't share openly in some of her previous church experiences. For her and so many others, words just aren't enough. They help, but they don't produce lasting transformation. What she needs most is loving presence—eyes that see her, arms that hug her, ears that listen to her, and hearts that love her in the here and now. She needs a new family, a safe family, a loving family, a healthy family. It's amazing to see what has happened over the past several years as she has experienced this tangible love. The rubble is being cleared, and her true dignity is emerging from the darkness.

WE ARE CALLED TO PARTICIPATE

We have a saying at The Refuge—*"healing won't drop out of the sky."* In other words, we aren't going to wake up tomorrow with all of our brokenness healed. As much as we'd love it to be that easy, transformation just doesn't work that way. Healing comes over a long period of time and through relationship with others. I am a huge proponent of the 12 Steps from *Alcoholics Anonymous* and their principles, based on the Beatitudes in Matthew 5:3-10, which guide the healing process. They understand that transformation takes a lifetime, and that we need to be with others on the same journey to gather strength and hope for the journey. They value the power of listening to each other's stories and gaining wisdom from those who have gone before us. Most of all, they recognize that without the combination of God and people, we will probably not find healing. We need both.

The church has a lot to learn from *Alcoholics Anonymous*. We must remember that restored dignity won't drop out of the sky. James and Sherrie won't wake up tomorrow feeling their true value and worth in the deepest places of their hearts, but they can over time.

We all need help from our friends. It reminds me of the story of Lazarus in John 11, when Jesus calls Lazarus back to life. He calls him out of the tomb, but then he looks to the people around him—his community, friends, and advocates—and says to them "unbind him" (v. 44). Unbind him. Unwrap him. Take off his graveclothes. I'll add my own words: *help shovel out the rubble so life can emerge again.*

I think God calls us to participate in this uncovering-unwrapping-unbinding-digging out process with each other through healing community.

And it takes a long time.

I can honestly say if I hadn't entered into a healing group 20 years ago and continued to show up week after week even when it's the last thing I wanted to do, I would still be completely buried underneath the rubble of my past. Growing up in an alcoholic home with depression, drugs, and abuse created a lot of shame for me. When I turned my life over to Jesus as a teenager, I had hoped all of these things would magically disappear. They didn't. When I rededicated my life as an adult, I hoped these things would magically disappear again. They didn't. Over the years I got mad about this because I felt like I had been promised something by the church that wasn't truthful. Over time, I learned that healing and restored dignity would be part of my ongoing spiritual development and would come not through attending more church services or grinding down on memorizing Bible passages or asking God for forgiveness one more time.

Instead, it would come through being with other women and men who were honest about their struggles and were trying to come back to life, too.

It would come through being with people who could "unbind me" while I at the same time participated in "unbinding them." In other words, it came through being with people who called out my dignity, who saw what I couldn't see, and who helped participate tangibly in clearing the rubble. They helped clear mine as I helped clear theirs, and over time, it has been amazing to see the life that has emerged. We've become more whole, more alive, more connected, more passionate, more engaged, more present, more free.

Now, twenty years later, I am more convinced than ever that the work of the church is to become dignity-restorers. We are called to participate together in community to help remove each other's grave clothes so that we can come to life so that God's image in each of us can emerge freely and fully. This is not easy work. It takes years and years, not months. And this is often a tough sell in a consumer-driven world where we like quick fixes and simple solutions.

But the path of Jesus was never supposed to be the easy road. In fact, the way of the cross is just the opposite. It is the harder path that leads to life and requires patience, endurance, humility, and grace. These are virtues that the church needs to keep developing and nurturing, especially in the long and laborious work of participating in calling people to life and restoring dignity where it's been lost. I've known James and Sherrie for years now, and much has been uncovered; but there's more rubble that needs excavating through ongoing healing community.

THE CHURCH IS CALLED TO BE DIGNITY-RESTORERS

Jesus restored dignity to people who had lost it—the sick, the lame, the broken, the desperate, the outcasts, the marginalized, the least, the last. Over and over, He healed them, lifted their heads, and touched them with hope. Hope that the Kingdom of God was available now and it wasn't only for the learned, the put-together, the well, and the powerful. It was available for all those who were humble enough to admit their spiritual poverty and need for God.

The world does not need any more dignity-strippers. What the world needs are patient, humble, and brave dignity-restorers:

- People who are willing to call out God's image in those that don't know it's there.
- People who are willing to sacrifice their own jobs, time, heart, and money to change systems that keep others oppressed.
- People who use their own power and privilege to make space for those without it.
- People who are willing to care about that one person who everyone else has given up on.
- People who see beyond gender, politics, religion, socioeconomics, and all of the other things that divide and segregate us and engage in deep and meaningful relationships anyway.
- People who are willing to go the long haul and offer compassion and love to the hurting instead of trite advice and easy spiritual answers.
- People who will stand between the stone throwers and the one about to be stoned and advocate on their behalf.
- People who touch the untouchable.
- People who see the best in others instead of the worst.

My hope and prayer for us as individuals, as people of God, is that we'd be known for these things. That people would see the church as a place that restores dignity and calls out everyone's inherent value and worth not with words but in actions. That we would bravely participate in each other's restoration.

If we were, more people like James and Sherrie would have a place to flourish, to have their value and worth be fanned into flame. They'd feel safe enough to tell their real stories. They'd learn to use their voice. They'd feel less alone. They'd be released of their shame. They would come to life.

Jesus says that the Kingdom of God is available to us now, and that part of our responsibility as Christ-followers is to participate in bringing heaven to earth. To me, that means we're called to be the lifter of heads, to be dignity restorers. To call each other to be all we were created to be. To nurture a spirit of equality, justice, mercy, love, and hope in the spaces and places we find ourselves in so that all can flourish. So that the "abundant life" that Jesus speaks about in John 10 could actually be realized.

God's work in our lives—and the work of the church—is to participate in calling out each other's dignity. I have no doubt if all our resources, hands, hearts, eyes, ears, buildings, power, influence, and hope could really be channeled to restoring dignity in person after person, the image of God uncovered in his people, shining brighter and brighter, would dim the darkness of this world like never before.

That's what I hope the church can be known for.

Section 5

PROCLAIMING SALVATION

{23}

A CHURCH THAT KNOWS ETERNAL LIFE IS BY GRACE ALONE THROUGH FAITH ALONE

By Jeremy Myers
Unless otherwise indicated, all Scripture references are from the NKJV.

When it comes to beliefs and behaviors that bring Christians together, there is nothing that unifies us more than the central Christian truth that eternal life is by grace alone, through faith alone, in Christ alone. Where grace and faith multiply, love and unity flourish. The degree that we emphasize grace and faith in our lives and in our community is the same degree to which we experience unity, peace, and harmony with God and with one another.

Grace and faith unite. When the Christian teaching about grace and faith are understood and put into practice, there is no greater unifying force within Christianity. Let us consider grace and faith to see why this is so.

227

GRACE ALONE

Grace is one of the central ideas which sets Christianity apart from all other belief systems in the world. While other groups may have some sort of teaching about forgiveness, the love and mercy of God, or a divine universal benevolence toward mankind, there is nothing quite like the Christian doctrine of grace. Nobody else believes that God loves us unconditionally, forgives us completely, and makes all His divine resources available to us with no strings attached.

This is why it is so shocking at times to see Christians stumble over each other in what sometimes seems to be a mad rush to abandon, limit, restrict, and tone down grace. In certain segments of Christianity there is a big debate about how much grace is too much. One side accuses the other of teaching "cheap grace" while another group prides itself in proclaiming "costly grace." Nobody wants to be accused of overdoing grace, or of extending too much grace. We want to talk about limiting grace, not allowing people to abuse grace, and making sure that grace is not viewed as a license to sin.

This is a move in the wrong direction. Rather than trying to limit and restrict grace, we should be tripping ourselves in the rush to proclaim the most radical, outrageous grace possible. If grace is central to Christianity, we should not be seeking to constrain, control, inhibit, and impede grace, but should be doing all we can to proclaim grace in all its shocking and scandalous clarity.

We must tell people in every possible way that God is not angry. That He loves us more than we can possibly imagine. That our good works contribute nothing to make God love us more. That God doesn't love some future "cleaned-up-obedient-got-it-all-together" version of us more than He loves us right now. That He accepts us just as we are. We are invited to the party. We are welcome to join the family, not because of how great we are, but because of how great He is.

With a God like this as our example, it is impossible to be too gracious. God is the champion of overdoing and overextending grace. God gives so much grace to those who don't deserve it, it borders on shameful. If any CEO tried to run a business the way God "runs" the world, the business would go bankrupt within a month. God lets people steal from Him (Luke 16:1-13), and show up late for work and still get paid (Matt 20:1-16). He hands out bonuses and gifts to both the good workers and the bad (Matt 5:45). When employees disobey all the company rules and regulations, He forgives them every time (Matt 18:21-22), even when they attempt to take over the company by killing His only Son (Matt 23:34).

Who behaves like this? Nobody! We have terms for people who behave this way. They are enablers. Over-permissive parents. Gullible fools who let others take advantage of them. If a person behaves this way as a judge or police officer, their behavior would be almost criminal.

And yet, this is the way God behaves every single day.

If Christians are going to follow the example of God, we have no business trying to put limits on limitless grace. If God wants to give something so scandalous to humanity, who are we to say He shouldn't? God knows that He will be taken advantage of and that people will use grace for their own selfish purposes. Apparently He doesn't care.

Or maybe, that is exactly the point. Maybe, in a world where nothing comes for free, where nobody loves without conditions, and where generosity toward others always has limits, in order for God to show people that He's serious about His love for us, He had to offer grace to its fullest extent (which is the only kind of grace there is). In order for people to notice grace as something only God can offer, it has be outrageous, shocking, and even scandalous. If it comes with conditions and fine print, the offer of grace from God is no different than anything else the world has to offer.

As you read this, you might be getting a bit nervous. The question you may be thinking is this: "So... does this mean that I can just go sin all I want?"

The best way to answer this question is with a simple answer: "Yes."

No ifs, ands, or buts. No qualifications. Just yes. God's grace is so outrageously shocking that it allows people to go sin all they want. Yes, God will still love and forgive them and extend His grace to them. If Christians want to follow God's example in extending grace, we have no business limiting it where He does not.

Yes, I know Paul answers the sin question a bit differently in Romans 6:1-2. But a careful reading of that text reveals that Paul never says that people *cannot* sin all they want, but that they *should not*. In Romans 6–8, Paul gives reasons why Christians should seek sanctification, but nowhere does He say that grace will cease if we sin too much. So have no fear, I agree with Paul. There are numerous reasons why we should not sin. Scripture reveals thousands of such reasons.

But nowhere does Scripture say that one reason we should not sin is because if we do, God will reject us, condemn us, stop loving us, or come to the end of His grace toward us. No, even if we sin, sin a lot, sin intentionally, and take advantage of grace to sin all we want, grace remains unmerited, free, infinite, and unconditionally extended. Grace cannot be exhausted, used up, limited, or restricted and still remain grace.

It is fine if pastors and Christian leaders want to warn people about sin. The Bible does and so should we. But let us never think that one of the tools at our disposal in the battle against sin is the threat of a limited supply of grace. Such a threat does not lead to obedience, but only to more sin. Even when such threats lead to life transformation, it is a transformation that comes not from a proper understanding of God, but from personal achievement and self-discipline, which only feed the sinful attitudes of pride, arrogance, and self-righteousness.

It is only grace—true grace, shocking, outrageous, unmerited, limitless grace—which can actually lead to true transformation of the life. Only when grace is understood as outlandish and unfathomable will our minds and souls be freed to live in the knowledge that we are loved, which is the only knowledge that leads to life. It is only grace that teaches us to deny ungodliness and worldly lusts, to help us live soberly, righteously, and godly in the present age (Titus 2:12).

Such talk of grace makes some uncomfortable. They think this takes grace too far. But again, with God as our example, nobody has ever taken grace too far. Though some have set sail on the ocean of God's grace and attempted to reach the other side, no sinner in human history has ever come close to laying eyes on that far shore.

How great is the Father's grace? To see, all we need to do is look at Jesus, and remind ourselves that "while we were still sinners, Christ died for us. ...For if when we were enemies we were reconciled to God through the death of His Son, much more, having been reconciled, we shall be saved by His life" (Rom 5:8, 10). It is a strange teaching in some Christian circles that God's grace is more effective on the unregenerate sinner than upon the redeemed and reconciled child of God. How could it be, asks Paul, that God's grace and love and forgiveness toward us would be less after we are justified than it was before? It cannot be! God sent His Son to die for us while we were yet sinners—while we were His enemies. But now, having been justified, having been adopted, regenerated, indwelled by the Spirit, and redeemed, does God's love and grace toward us now diminish in power and glory? Of course not! If anything, it is magnified toward us, in us, and through us. If God "did not spare His own Son, but delivered Him up for us all, how shall He not with Him also freely give us all things?" (Rom 8:32).

So enough of this talk about taking grace too far, of cheap grace vs. costly grace, and of reaching the limits of God's grace. There is no such thing. Grace, true grace, is one of the keys to vibrant Christianity and unity within the church. We will see how grace leads to unity after a brief look at faith.

FAITH ALONE

If outrageous grace is a central unifying Christian truth, its twin is pure, unadulterated faith. Yet while true grace is uniquely Christian; faith is not. All people have faith. Every religion centers on ideas that people must believe. Even atheists believe they have enough knowledge about the universe to know that there is no God.

Nevertheless, although everyone has faith, there is something unique about Christian faith. And what makes Christian faith unique cannot begin to be grasped until we first understand grace. It is not an overstatement to say that the less a person understands grace, the less they will understand faith. Specifically, if a person thinks that God's love and forgiveness is somewhat dependent on their good behavior, they will think that the way we receive God's love and forgiveness is also somewhat dependent upon good behavior. But as soon as we grasp the infinite and absolute freeness of God's grace, it is only then that we begin to grasp that faith has nothing to do with good works, but is the exact opposite of works (Rom 4:5). By faith, we simply receive the good gift which has been offered. But if we think the gift of eternal life is somehow dependent upon our behavior, then we will also think that something more than faith is needed to obtain that gift.

Of course, just as some people object to unapologetic teaching about grace, so also, many object to a strong stance on faith alone. The objections are numerous, ranging from "you will know them by their fruit" (Matt 7:16), to "faith without works is dead," and "even the demons believe" (Jas 2:17, 19). So just as with grace, Christians have a bad habit of seeing who can most quickly alter the freeness of eternal life to all who simply and only believe.

We want to talk about head faith, heart faith, true faith, spurious faith, persevering faith, transforming faith, and all sorts of other qualifiers for faith which Scripture never uses. We even say things like "Salvation is by faith alone, but not by a faith that is alone." Logically and theologically, such statements make no sense, and have little to defend them in Scripture. If God offers eternal life to all who believe, who are we to amend this offer with our own conditions, qualifications, and requirements? Those verses which seem to teach additional requirements and conditions beyond faith alone in Jesus Christ actually teach the exact opposite when studied in their various contexts (none of which we have room to dissect in this chapter).

However, logic also reveals that faith must be truly alone if it is to remain faith. When the radical grace of God is grasped in all its glory, only then do we begin to see that there can be no condition to receiving God's grace other than simply believing in Jesus for it.

So like grace alone, faith alone also is a radical Christian idea. Faith teaches us that there is nothing we can say or do to earn favor with God. Faith reminds us that God is not angry, but wants all to accept His invitation into His family. Faith shows us that God knows us better than we know ourselves. God knows that if He made any small fraction of our eternal life dependent upon human frailty and weakness, none would receive eternal life. Faith tells us that the only thing God desires from us is to accept all that He has already done for us through Jesus Christ.

LIVING LIVES OF GRACE AND FAITH

Once we embrace the concepts of outrageous grace and pure, unadulterated faith as the means by which God grants eternal life to us, we begin to see that this is also how God wants us to behave toward other people.

We are to extend grace and forgiveness toward others until it becomes shameful. We are to love others as God has loved us. We are to overlook the wrongs and faults in others, trusting that God will work in their lives in His way at His own time just as He patiently works in ours. We can believe this just as we are accepted by God on the basis of nothing but His grace. As ambassadors of the grace of God, we also can accept others on the basis of nothing but God's grace. Other people don't need to conform to our personal list of rules or regulations to be accepted or loved by us. They can simply be accepted. By faith, we can trust that God will work in their lives through Scripture, the Holy Spirit, and the fellowship of others. Our only task is to view others in the same way God views them—as people of unsurpassable worth, so loved and valued by God that He sent His Son to die for them.

Understanding God's grace helps us practice grace toward others. Grace extends patience to those who believe and behave differently than we do. Grace understands that not every doctrine is a hill to die on, and so we can get along with people who disagree. Grace even extends forgiveness toward those who consistently disappoint us and even have long-standing habits of sin. Through grace, we can see that we do not have to fix everyone of everything, but that God, through the work of the Holy Spirit and in His own time, will help that sinning brother or sister through their issues just as God has done with us. Grace keeps us from trying to be God to other people so that we can simply love them as God does.

Understanding the simplicity of faith also liberates us to view others differently. When we begin to understand that God's gift of eternal life is received by faith, it is then that we begin to believe in God for other things, such as His ability to deal with the sin and problems of other people. Again, most of Christianity seems to have a God-complex where we want to fix the sin in other people (while blindly ignoring the sin in our own lives). But faith toward God allows us to also put faith in God toward other people. That is, by faith in God, we can believe the best about people. We can hope for something better. We can dream of how relationships and fellowship can improve. Faith helps us imagine something better for our broken marriages, rebellious children, and damaged friendships, and enables us to seek for ways to bring hope and healing into these relationships.

We can, by faith, view people the way God sees them, as people who are infinitely valuable and worth dying for. Without faith, it is impossible to see Jesus in the face of an AIDS-stricken homeless man who is sleeping in his own filth; however, by faith, we can behold the glory of the Son of Man who emptied Himself and became human to love, serve, and honor people just like this homeless man… and just like me.

Grace and faith unite. They help us see what God is like, and how God wants us to live here on earth as His ambassadors and representatives. Radical, outrageous, shocking grace is what the world needs, along with men and women of vibrant, unadulterated, imaginative faith who God uses to reveal His grace to the world. When we go forth in such grace and faith, we go forward united with God and with one another, and in so doing, unite heaven and earth into the Kingdom of God.

{24}

A CHURCH THAT SEES
EVERY CHRISTIAN AS A
BROTHER OR SISTER

By Christopher Dryden
Unless otherwise indicated, all Scripture references are from the NIV.

*Keep on loving one another as brothers and
sisters (Heb 13:1).*

The Bible uses numerous metaphors to describe the church. For example, it could be a Bride, a Body, or a Building. Each picture helps give a better understanding of the role and responsibility of the church. In looking at the church as a family, the word family is not a tool used to describe what the church is like; rather, this is what the church is—a family. This concept has been an integral part of human relations since creation. This chapter explores how that family feeling affects relations both in and out of that glorious family.

JESUS AND HIS BRETHREN

Jesus Christ's incarnation reinforces the importance of family connections since He came as both the Son of Man and the Son of God. His ministry also did more than anything to shape how we are to engage with each other, namely in familial terms.

In teaching His disciples to pray, Jesus starts with those two words—Our Father. This established their relationship with the God of the universe as One who is our source. Referring to Him as Father, Jesus clearly makes us brothers and sisters.

In Matthew 12:46-50, Jesus relates to those who follow Him as brothers and sisters more than His flesh and blood relatives. This again lets us know that joining the family of God means something different happens to relational dynamics. We are not *like* brothers and sisters—we *are* brothers and sisters because of our connection with Jesus. His connection with the Father makes us all a part of the same family in the closest way.

Further reiterating our family status, Matthew 23:8-9 shows Jesus marking out how we are supposed to consider each other as brothers with one Father in heaven. There is equality among us as brothers and sisters.

Both the one who makes people holy and those who are made holy are of the same family. So Jesus is not ashamed to call them brothers and sisters (Heb 2:11).

Paul puts it simply that the plan was for Jesus to be the first of many brothers and sisters (Rom 8:29); we are all made a part of the family because of God's plan from the beginning of time. That there are frequent references to the audience of various epistles, as brothers and sisters, further confirms the status we take on because of Christ. Even a casual reader of the New Testament picks up on the theme of family and believers as brothers and sisters.

YOU ARE MY BROTHER; YOU ARE MY SISTER. SO WHAT?

Jesus outlines clearly that we are to see ourselves as brothers and sisters. Yet in a fractured world where some sibling relationships bear great resemblance to Cain and Abel, what does that mean?

Jesus exemplifies the sort of sibling relationship He expects among believers. His relationship with His disciples demonstrates humility, empowering, equipping, enabling, and ultimately a sacrificial love for His brothers and sisters. Christ expects them to replicate these things upon His departure. Indeed His prayer for unity in John 17 was intrinsically based on a relationship of brothers loving each other that would be a declaration to the world of the Father who sent the Son.

The glorious picture we get of the church soon after Jesus ascends is one marked by a love for each other. The outpouring of the Holy Spirit on Pentecost evidently sparked the initial expression of this love. This could be seen both in generous giving to those in need and in a desire to share life by receiving teaching from the apostles and enjoying each other's company in sharing meals. The bond that tied them together was a deep abiding spiritual love that helped them see each other as brother and sister.

This love for the brethren is evidently not a shallow or superficial affair. Here is love that crosses into the personal effects of life. Here is love that thrives on regular interaction. It is something that goes beyond presence and contact, entering into engagement and intimacy in obedience to Jesus' command to love each other as He loved us.

This is not to give the impression that the early church was perfect. Neither is it to suggest that this expression of love and sense of belonging to the family is something lost in the 21st Century.

MODERN EXPRESSIONS OF BROTHERLY LOVE

Drew (not his real name) and I had met through the YMCA. I was employed there as a development worker responsible for engaging with the residents of the hostel on Christian issues in creative ways. Drew is a comedian on the circuit, who is also a Christian. He had been recommended by my boss to run some comedy workshops.

As it transpired we were able to develop a good relationship (despite the fact that we were two people who had not previously known each other and whose church backgrounds would not have seen us mix in the same circles). Yet here we were putting on activities that could help young people develop their confidence and a greater awareness of who they are.

We developed a relationship with each other that was a good impression of the same brotherly love talked about in Scripture. It got to the stage that for a season we would gather regularly at his home with other brothers and sisters in Christ from various church backgrounds. We had a great sense of freedom to be ourselves without any masks or pretense.

As we treated each other as family, no one was considered greater than anyone else. We valued each other's input, and there was a liberty in sharing not just verbally, but also materially. If there was a need and we could meet it, we would do so without a second thought. As with the early church, this was not a blissful, perfect haven free of conflict and strife. There were tensions. Some disagreements could have become toxic and jeopardized body unity, but this did not happen because there was an underlying value of each other as brothers and sisters in Christ. That meant more than anything.

The apostle John wrote just how important it is to treat fellow disciples as brothers and sisters, stating that if we don't love the brother we can see, then we cannot make a claim to love the God we cannot see. Likewise failing to love that sister suggests that the love of God is not in us.

This underlies a crucial point: the foundation for any expression of love for those outside the family is the love we have in the family. The world will we know we are truly followers of Christ as we let brotherly love continue.

WHAT ABOUT NON-CHRISTIANS?

The motor that drives us to consider non-Christians as potential brothers and sisters is our brother Jesus taking that approach with us. Paul says it best in Romans that while we were yet sinners, Christ died for us. That is to say, while we rebelled against Him, He died for us.

So as recipients of such unmerited love, our perspectives on others change. The love of Christ compels us to engage with non-Christians with the same love. This is why in Matthew 25, Jesus states that the sheep will be welcomed into the Kingdom because of what they did to those who Jesus calls the least of His brothers and sisters.

In Matthew 5, Jesus says what marks us out as children of the Father is our ability to show such love to even our enemies. We love non-Christians because we are assured that this is how children of God behave. Even those who oppose us or find our faith irrelevant are viewed not as the enemy, but as an opportunity to overcome evil with good.

This is about seeing what God wanted from the beginning—to have a people who live in praise and adoration of Him and in sharing that love with others. Sin does not have

241

the final answer in the human condition. The redemptive work of Jesus Christ means that while there's life there's hope, and as witnesses of the hope as seen in our own transformed lives, we dare not engage with non-Christians as though their plight is utterly hopeless.

The Gospel message is centered on the mission of the Son of God who came to seek and save the lost. As people who have been found, our treatment of those who are still lost is to be concerned for them as we would a perishing sibling. That perspective adjusts how we engage with non-Christians.

The church does not consider non-Christians as targets or numbers to get in church buildings. As potential members of the family, we engage with them in loving and compassionate ways in the hope that they too will enjoy what we have enjoyed and so become a part of the family.

What allows us to view things from this perspective is an understanding of how we are brought into the family of God, namely by grace through the saving work of Jesus Christ. Paul in his letter of Ephesians stresses that we are in the family not because our works, but because of grace. We believe that Christ did everything. There's no room for boasting.

REASON FOR A CHANGE IN PERSPECTIVE

The propulsion power of the mission can be seen in a personal story.

I grew up with a very insular attitude. My perspective was that I was brought up in a church that got it right. That means I got it right. As I got it right, then those who didn't agree got it wrong. This meant that at best I engaged on cordial terms when I had to with Christians of different persuasions.

My attitude was a lot worse toward the sinners. These people were to be pitied. Their lifestyles were so degrading that we simply avoided them. This was not about cutting off from society, but keeping the barriers clear between engaging with them at work or wherever, and what I did in my own time. As far as I was concerned the sinners needed saving, and I could do that by giving them a booklet about their need for Jesus and that was it.

THE CHURCH AND COMMUNITY—CONTEXT FOR CHANGE

This attitude came to a head when I lived in Stoke-on-Trent. I was part of a church plant that wanted to establish itself as a part of the fabric of the community. This was about loving our neighbors. This was about Good Samaritan living. You meet the need you see—sharing life with others and serving them. This was also sharing our need for support as well. It was all new and scary for me.

At one point we held some of our gatherings at the local YMCA hostel. This was a place known for its residents being young people messed up emotionally, psychologically, and in some cases physically. Sexual, alcohol, and drug abuse were common. The stench of some of the residents suggested their priority didn't include hygiene. Meeting there used to make me physically uncomfortable. I would be glad to get out as quickly as possible because I didn't want to be associated with such an unpleasant clientele.

Soon after we finished holding meetings there, my attitude was challenged with a number of serious personal set-backs. In it, God was saying that if I thought the residents of the YMCA were smelly and unclean then it was time I looked in the mirror. As I did so, by the help of the Spirit, I saw how my own attitude was disgusting to God. I truly did not appreciate the work of Christ on the cross. His sacrifice broke down barriers and gave access to anyone to have fellowship with Him.

This humbling process brought a turnaround in my behavior. I was encouraged to see people from the perspective of Jesus. He did not show condescending pity to those in a helpless condition. He took upon Himself the body of flesh. He lived with us, sharing in our experiences. Christ indicated the way to God, which wasn't about ostracizing. This was about embracing all of who God is and what His mission of redemption was all about.

THE HARVEST IS RIPE—YOU ARE THE LABORER OF LOVE

> When he saw the crowds, he had compassion on them, because they were harassed and helpless, like sheep without a shepherd. Then he said to his disciples, "The harvest is plentiful but the workers are few. Ask the Lord of the harvest, therefore, to send out workers into his harvest field" (Matt 9:36-39).

I now saw that the correct approach to interacting with non-Christians was to be moved with compassion as Jesus was. Our Lord commissioned His followers to get on with the task of proclaiming the Kingdom that makes right that which is wrong.

The move to compassion came full circle when the "horrible" YMCA turned out to be the place where I worked next as the development worker. It was Jesus, full of compassion and mercy, who challenged me to see each individual as fearfully and wonderfully made—a potential sibling.

The transformation work enabled me to get involved with the mission in the compassionate manner that God expects from His children.

CONCLUSION: A FAMILY PERSPECTIVE

In the beginning the Father and Son created all that is. It delighted the Father to do so for His Son. It delighted the Son to return glory back to the Father. By His Spirit, He created humanity to reflect this love among each other. Though sin has endeavored to distort the picture, God's redemption story has brought it right back on track. Now the Family of God demonstrating true brotherly love shares that with those who are yet to know Him. As this happens, we anticipate the return of the Son for the glory of the Father.

{25}

A CHURCH THAT PROCLAIMS THE GOSPEL IN AN UNDERSTANDABLE WAY

By Jeremy Myers
Unless otherwise indicated, all Scripture references are from the NKJV.

It is sadly ironic that one of the most divisive elements within the church is that which was intended to create the greatest unity. What element is that? The Gospel.

The Gospel of God was given to tear down the dividing walls of hostility, to destroy the racial, religious, economic, political, and gender divisions between Jew and Gentile, rich and poor, master and slave, and men and women (Gal 3:28; Eph 2:14). Yet for some reason, the Gospel often seems to create an ever-increasing number of divisions and factions within Christianity. Somehow, the Gospel of unity, the Gospel of peace, the Gospel of forgiveness, grace, and mercy, has become a warzone in which every battle is fought to the bloody death.

But this chapter is going to end the age-old war for the Gospel once and for all. Once a person reads this essay, they will never again go to war over the Gospel.

I jest, of course.

I do, however, think that some of what is proposed in this chapter can bring unity and understanding to some of the warring factions. Though complete unity on the Gospel may never be possible this side of glory, we can move toward unity by understanding a few things about this Gospel over which we vehemently battle. Simply by grasping a few foundational truths of the Gospel, there can be peace between Calvinists and Arminians, peace between proponents of Lordship Salvation and Free Grace, peace between mainstream liberals and evangelical conservatives, and peace between members of Westboro Baptist Church and everyone else. ...Well, maybe not that last one.

Hopefully, as Christians of all backgrounds, beliefs systems, and behaviors come to agreement on three foundational truths of the Gospel, we will naturally begin to grow into the unity of the faith, and proclaim the Gospel in such a way that promotes this unity among all who follow Jesus. But before we can proclaim the Gospel in a way that promotes unity, we must understand the Gospel as a message of unity.

GOSPEL PEACE

The first foundational truth of the Gospel is that it is a Gospel of peace. The Gospel was intended to advance and promote peace. Not just peace to our inner beings, and not just peace between men and God, but also peace between all people and eventually, ultimately, peace to the entire universe.

In one of the first declarations of the Gospel in the Bible, the angels announce the birth of Jesus to shepherds and proclaim to them peace on earth and goodwill toward men (Luke

2:10, 14). Throughout the entire ministry of Jesus, He sought to bring peace where there was hostility, and love where there was hate. Even among the twelve apostles, Jesus brought together zealots and tax collectors who would have hated each other in any other context. Near the end of His ministry, Jesus proclaimed to His apostles that He had come to bring peace, was leaving them with His peace (John 14:27), and that just as God had sent Jesus to proclaim peace, so also, His followers must do the same (John 20:21). In the letters of Paul and Peter it is the same. Over and over, these apostolic writers proclaim that in Jesus Christ, there is now peace (e.g., Eph 2:14-17; Col 1:20; 1 Pet 3:11).

As such, any time we use the Gospel to produce anything but peace, we are misusing and abusing the Gospel. If our defense of the Gospel causes bitterness, strife, and division "for the sake of the Gospel," it is likely that we do not understand or defend the true Gospel of peace in Jesus Christ.

But what about when Jesus claims He did not come to bring peace, but a sword, that His ministry would not result in peace, but division (cf. Matt 10:34; Luke 12:51)? Sadly, these statements by Jesus have been severely misused by Christians who want to justify their own warlike behavior toward other Christians. Such a view, however, contradicts almost everything else Jesus taught. It is best, therefore, to understand that Jesus is not talking about His *purpose* in coming, but rather, a consequence of His ministry and teaching. His statement is not prescriptive, but descriptive. He is not describing what He *wanted* to happen, but rather, is describing what *would* happen. This is not a statement of desire or intention by Jesus, but is a statement of realistic understanding about what might occur as people follow Him.

In speaking of a sword, Jesus is using hyperbole and exaggeration to make the point that as a result of what He taught, there would be strife and division among people; yes, even among family members. This was not the goal and was not ideal, but Jesus realistically understood that such divisions would occur.

Jesus desired, intended, and prayed for peace among all men, but He knew that as a result of what He was teaching, there would be some discord and dissention. The statement of Jesus should be read with a tone of sadness in His voice, not an air of excited anticipation. Jesus is not saying, "Let's go cut off the heads of everyone who disagrees with me!" but rather, "I am deeply saddened by the fact that people will use my words and my teachings to go to war with their brethren. I know the hearts of men, and some will abuse my example and my teaching in just this way. For some, my words will not lead to peace, but to a sword." Jesus did not want to bring a sword, strife, discord, and war, but knew that some would twist and pervert His words and His ways to justify evil actions such as these.

From first to last, the Gospel is a message of peace. Therefore, those who teach, preach, and live the Gospel will be known as men and women of peace. They will be known for their love and service toward others. They will be known for their unity.

But the Gospel as a message of peace is not the only element of the Gospel that promotes unity. The Gospel also promotes unity when we understand that the Gospel is a parody.

GOSPEL PARODY

Though the events surrounding the Gospel are historically accurate, they are also satirical polemics. Using the life and ministry of Jesus, the Gospel mocks Caesar and any human lordling who would set himself up as the one who will bring peace and justice to the world. This satirical element to the

Gospel is seen in a variety of ways throughout the New Testament.

Take the four Gospels themselves. Many people today do not realize that "Gospel" was a specific genre of literature in the first century Roman Empire. Every time a new Caesar came to power, he would have Gospel accounts written about himself and then distributed throughout the empire. The Caesar Gospels included stories about how the new Caesar was born, how he grew up, and some of the superhuman miracles he performed during his life. The Caesar Gospels usually included promises about how the new Caesar was the "Son of God" who would bring peace to the entire world, and how as a result, every Roman citizen must proclaim Caesar as Lord.

One can easily see that in such an environment, the Gospels about Jesus written by Matthew, Mark, Luke, and John would be viewed as potentially treasonous. These four Gospels were making the claim that Caesar was not Lord; Jesus Christ was Lord. That Caesar would not bring peace; but Jesus Christ introduced peace to the world. That Caesar's divine birth, wise teachings, and miraculous events were mere myth, but such things really did happen in the life, ministry, and teaching of Jesus Christ.

Using true history as a parody, the Gospel writers called into question all the central beliefs and practices of Roman life and worship, and called people away from Caesar worship and into a politically and culturally subversive life with Jesus Christ.

The four Gospels are not alone in using satire, polemic, and parody to contrast the Gospel of Jesus Christ with all other claims and promises of political and religious leaders. Paul's letter to the Romans, for example, also begins with parody. The opening paragraphs of this letter make a farcical mockery of Caesar and his empty claims to bring peace and justice to all. In a time when every Roman Caesar claimed to be god's divine representative on earth (even claiming the title Son of God), Paul courageously writes a letter to the Christians in the capital city of the Roman Empire and makes the bold claim that in Jesus Christ, the true Gospel of the true Son of God has been revealed, and in it, the true and lasting justice of God has been revealed to all men (cf. Rom 1:3-4, 16-17).

We could go book by book through the New Testament, showing how the authors of Scripture spoke of the Gospel in a way that both mocked and trumped the proud and foolish claims of political and religious leaders of that day. Such a survey would reveal that the goals and aspirations of politics and religion are usually not wrong, but the means and methods by which political and religious leaders seek to accomplish these goals are way off base. The Gospel shows believers how to live before a watching world so that the greatest dreams of humanity come to fruition in our very midst.

In this way, we get our first glimpse of how the Gospel helps Christians grow into unity with one another. When we understand that the New Testament (indeed, the entire Bible!) mocks the power struggles of worldly-minded men, our eyes begin to see the proud and petty power struggles that exist in our own life. The Gospel challenges our own quests for personal prominence, recognition, and fame. The Gospel lays bare the motivations of our heart to reveal that many of our battles over the Gospel are little more than struggles for control between power-hunger people.

When we begin to see that the Gospel turns power on its head, mocks and makes fun of people who exert their own prominence and destroy others to protect their own positions of authority, it is then that we begin to understand that there is more to following Jesus than being right, being up front, and being the leader. We begin to honor others above ourselves. We begin to listen more than we talk. We begin to serve more than seek to be served. As we do these things, we look around one day and discover that we have grown in unity with one another, much to our delight.

GOSPEL DELIGHT

The delight we experience as we live out the Gospel among our friends, family, and neighbors is actually part of the Gospel as well. The Gospel, when properly understood and practiced, becomes a great source of present joy and delight. This is because the Gospel is not just about the "by and by," but also about the "here and now." The Gospel message is intended to create delight in life, not just to alleviate concerns about what happens after death. The Gospel is not just about going to heaven when we die, but is also about experiencing heaven while we live. The Gospel is not just a message of hope for the dying, but is a message of delight for those who want to live. It does not call us to "Keep looking up" for the blessed return of our Lord and Savior Jesus Christ, but to keep looking out for ways that we can incarnate the return of Jesus in our very lives to those we interact with every day. The Gospel is not about waiting until we die or Jesus returns, but is about doing all we can to live our lives in such a way that Jesus returns in us.

I think it was Robert Farrar Capon who once said that while many Christians cannot wait to die so they can be gloried, God cannot wait for us to start living so He can be glorified. This is exactly the truth of the Gospel. The Gospel is about how to live here and now so we look like Jesus and practice the principles of the Kingdom of God. When this happens, light, love, peace, and hope shine through our lives into the hopeless despair and darkness in which so many people live.

So when we live within the Gospel of delight, we live our lives here and now with as much joy, love, contentment, service, and grace toward others as we possibly can. When we live in such ways, our lives become a vision of what heaven will be like. Our lives point people to the reality of what God intends for the world. We become a picture of what God desires for all people, a waking dream of what we might become.

True unity among Christians who disagree on the Gospel (and many other issues) can only begin to develop when we see that the Gospel is not just about believing certain propositions, but also about behaviors put into practice. The Gospel unveils a way of life for the here and now so that all who believe and follow the Gospel can live, love, and look like Jesus to a dark and dying world.

PROCLAIMING GOSPEL UNITY

Once we begin to understand how the Gospel creates peace, mocks our vain claims to self-importance, and teaches us to live as agents of joy and delight in the world, how can these truths be proclaimed in a way that creates unity among the bickering factions of Christianity?

Let me propose four ways to proclaim the Gospel in a way that promotes unity among all followers of Jesus:

First, the Gospel teaches us that truth is only true if carried out in love. While we can agree that there is no love without truth, it is essential for doctrinally-minded Christians to remember that there also is no truth without love. True truth will always express itself in love. If you are warring and fighting with your brother, especially over doctrine, it is probably a good indication that you have misunderstood the truth.

So when we proclaim the Gospel, let us teach the truth in a loving way. Let us make sure our words and actions drip with love and grace. When others disagree (and there will be disagreement, for unity is not uniformity), let us seek not to offend and accuse those with whom we disagree, but to probe and ask questions in a way that allows us to understand their perspective and invites them to see things from our perspective. Name calling and labeling people as heretics is never okay in such conversations.

Second, an accurate proclamation of the Gospel can bring unity to the various sides of the "works vs. faith" debate when we understand the Gospel as an all-encompassing message about what we believe *and* how we live. The "works vs. faith" debate has raged over whether or not the Gospel requires works as a way to earn, keep, or prove one's eternal life. Yet as we have briefly seen, this debate comes from a simple categorical mistake of confusing a small part of the Gospel with its entirety. If two people are arguing about what qualifies as true "fruit" and one has apples in mind and the other has oranges, but they keep using the world "fruit" the argument quickly becomes quite messy. Gospel debates are like that. The Gospel is a wide-ranging message about what God has done for the entire world through the life, teachings, crucifixion, death, burial, and resurrection of Jesus Christ. It not only contains truths about how a person can go to heaven when they die, but also about how a follower of Jesus can live here on earth. So if one person is thinking only about the parts of the Gospel that tell a person how to go to heaven when they die (faith alone in Christ alone), and another person is thinking about the parts of the Gospel which tell followers of Jesus how to live on this earth (discipleship, obedience, faithful living), but both persons keep using the term "Gospel," well, the argument quickly becomes quite messy.

So when we proclaim the Gospel, let us emphasize *both* the elements of the Gospel that we must believe *and* the elements of the Gospel that we must practice. In this way, we can agree with those who proclaim that eternal life is a free gift of God to all who simply and only believe in Jesus for it, and we can agree with those who proclaim that the Gospel calls us to live radically different lives than what is seen in the world around us. Such agreement with both sides of the debate is not inconsistent with the full-orbed message of the Gospel.

Third, once we see that the Gospel contains a whole host of truths and doctrines to believe and teach *and also* a broad spectrum of behaviors to practice and obey, our proclamation of the Gospel can bring unity between all types of churches and approaches to ministry. It is often common to hear some churches and groups of believers emphasizing the importance of Bible study and expository sermons, while other churches and groups of believers emphasize social action and community service. The two groups often view each other with suspicion, thinking that the other group is neglecting central truths of the Gospel.

However, a proclamation of the all-encompassing message of the Gospel—with a healthy view of the universal nature of the church (discussed elsewhere in this book)—allows for one group of believers to focus on teaching, learning, Bible study, and theology, while another group of believers focuses on service, acts of mercy, and community outreach. One is not necessarily better than the other; both are needed for the Body of Christ to fully proclaim the Gospel to the watching world, and each group can praise the other for doing what they themselves are not. Those who believe Christians should be listening to more sermons and attending more Bible studies can nod and smile toward those who prefer to be out feeding the poor and tending the sick, and vice versa. Both sides recognize that if they are truly following the Gospel, there will come a time when their roles must reverse, or at least become more balanced. There is a time to study, and a time to serve; a time to learn, and a time to love.

Ultimately, a proper Gospel proclamation will remind us that no matter what, we are all one family. And just like any family, there will be internal disagreements, struggles, and arguments. There may need to be some discipline that takes place, some separations that must occur. But when these arguments and breakups happen, the Gospel teaches that we are still family, and that despite our hurt feelings, theological disagreements, and interfamily strife, the goal of the Gospel is reconciliation and redemption, not just of each of us to one another, but ultimately and eventually, the redemption and reconciliation of all things under the Lordship of Jesus Christ. Though the Gospel brings unity, it does not bring uniformity. The Gospel does not create clones, but creates a multifaceted family, full of vibrant color, unique perspectives, and multidimensional ministries. The Gospel is so versatile and wideranging, it is a "one-size-fits-all" message for people who are anything but "one-size-fits-all."

None of this means that the development of unity through the proclamation of the Gospel is easy. In fact, unity is a bit like humility: both vanish the moment you think you've achieved it. Unity, like humility, can never be our goal. Unity is a byproduct of living within the Gospel. Unity occurs naturally as a result of following Jesus as He leads us into peace with God and each other, into a gentle mocking of our own pride and ambition, and into a full-fledged delight at the beauty and wonder of life in this world.

When viewed this way, the Gospel is a truth that binds us all together in unity, whether we are high church or low church, mega church or house church, or some mixture in between. The Gospel is not something that divides, but unites, and brings us together into the unity of the faith no matter how different and diverse we may be.

{26}

A CHURCH THAT TAKES
THE GOSPEL TO THE ENDS
OF THE EARTH

By Miguel Labrador
Unless otherwise indicated, all Scripture references are from the NASB.

It must be decided whether or not the Gospel can, in fact, be hindered. If the Gospel *is* the *power* of *God* unto salvation for those that believe (Rom 1:16), then it's fair to ask, "What can stand in the way of God's power?" The most natural answer is "Nothing." That said, I believe it's entirely plausible that the church can impede the *taking* of the Gospel to the ends of the earth. Rather than producing another list of angry words, criticisms, or complaints about what the church is doing wrong, and in keeping with the tone of this book, I'll endeavor to describe the characteristics of a church that lets the Gospel flow.

Unlike messengers delivering secret dispatches in times of war, we are not only permitted, but also encouraged to know the contents of the message we carry. The Gospel is primarily a message. The purpose of that message is that the eyes of

259

hearts may be enlightened in order to know the hope to which Jesus has called His people (Eph 1:18). In 1 Corinthians 15:18, the apostle Paul summarizes the most basic components of the Gospel message, namely, the death, burial, resurrection, and appearances of the resurrected Christ. The message can never be separated from the man Christ Jesus (1 Tim 2:5). In the book *Scripture As Logos: Rabbi Ishmael and the Origins of Midrash*, the author points out that, "The logos is simultaneously the instructor and the content of its instruction." If that is true, then the Gospel is both The Word / *Logos* (Jesus) and His words / *logois* (Luke 23:9; Luke 4:22).

Jesus is mediator, messenger, and message of the Gospel. A local church that hesitates in the transmission of the Gospel usually does so because of not being familiar with the message's contents. And so, we're decidedly for:

THE GOSPEL'S MOVING PARTS

Did you know the Gospel has moving parts that help us stay on mission? It does. These moving parts are:

- *A Gospel that originates in the triune nature of God, the One in whom we live and move and have our being* (Acts 17:28). It includes the Gospel of Christ (Mark 1:1; Rom 1:9; 1 Cor 9:12), the Gospel of the Holy Spirit (1 Thess 1:5), and the Gospel of the Father (Rom 11:28).

- *A Gospel that perpetuates grace* (Acts 20:24). It emphasizes that salvation in all of its aspects is on the basis of grace rather than on some meritorious system of works.

- *A Gospel that communicates and confirms the Kingdom* (Matt 4:23; 9:35; 24:14). It is the good news that

God will establish His Kingdom on earth as it is in heaven.

- *A Gospel that establishes and authenticates peace* (Eph 6:15). It describes how this good news of salvation in Christ brings peace in all its many aspects (peace with God, the peace of God, and peace with others) through the victory accomplished by the Savior.

- *A Gospel that calls for the recognition of eternity placed within human hearts* (Eccl 3:11). It's an aspect of the Gospel that expands our perspective as we normally think of it (Rev 14:6).

- *A Gospel that saves* (1 Cor 15:2; Eph 1:13). I've put this last in the list because it's often first, and in fact, the only Gospel that the church preaches. "The Gospel of Salvation," in truth, may be the least mentioned aspect of the Biblically robust Gospel message. I'll leave that to you. These six moving parts of the Gospel are those, that if preserved, will keep it in motion and unhindered.

To some, the difference between hindering the Gospel and hindering the spread of the Gospel might be negligible. I don't think it is. The Gospel is the power of God (Rom 1:16). The church has been given the authority, ability, and credibility to propagate it. That credibility is rooted in the coming of Jesus, His subsequent life, death, resurrection, and eternality. He and His Gospel confirm the faith. The Gospel continually reveals the manifold nature of God's righteousness (Rom 1:17). One doesn't "preach the Gospel" and then go on to others things. God will never cease to be manifold. The Gospel is multidimensional in purpose and scope. Unnecessarily constricting the Gospel to suit our short-term and often short-sighted goals can impede its eternal migratory nature.

My wife and I are missionaries in the most commonly understood use of the word "missionary." We have been situated in the Andes Mountains Cloud Forest Region of Ecuador for over eight years. This region of Ecuador is called a "megadiverse" for its biological and cultural diversity. This exists primarily because of pocketed communities spread throughout the mountainous region. In these pockets, sub-cultures have emerged and have been preserved. Many of these micro-cultures have their own histories and stories. They have unique ways of understanding things. They use slightly different words to convey their thoughts. They move differently, aspire to things differently, and assume differently than their neighbors who might be just over the next hill.

As of the writing of this chapter, we are working in 29 different communities, attempting to continually take the Gospel to them and guiding them in the taking of it to their surrounding communities. We have been asked many times to describe our "method" and to give reasons for our "success." We've also been asked directly, "Why aren't we seeing the same growth that you guys are in Ecuador?" There are various reasons why this might be, but eventually it nearly always comes down to the Gospel message and the manner in which it's being preached.

PARTICIPATION IN THE GOSPEL

The Apostle Paul had deeply intimate relationships with many across a wide geographical area. That intimacy came from a bond that was birthed in the "joining in" of the work of God in the world. It was the advancement of the Gospel, the making of disciples, and the engagement of mission that united them and fostered participation in it. It was "participating" in the Gospel that empowered them to live it.

262

The apostle Paul wrote to the Philippians (modern day Macedonia):

> I thank my God in all my remembrance of you, always offering prayer with joy in my every prayer for you all, in view of your participation in the Gospel from the first day until now. For I am confident of this very thing, that He who began a good work in you will perfect it until the day of Christ Jesus (Php 1:3-6).

The Philippians assumed that they were to join in, or participate in, the propagation of the Gospel from the very beginning. How did they know? I believe it was because the preaching of the Gospel to them included the idea of its propagation by them. In other words, they knew from the first day that they were supposed to be partakers in the mission and not just purveyors of it.

I'm still amazed when I come across believers that truly think that Gospel work is solely for professionals, full-time ministers, or clergy. This is confirmed and perpetuated when most of what is heard regarding the Gospel comes from non-participatory pulpit preaching. If the Gospel you're preaching isn't self-propagating, and if it always "depends" on you, then it's likely you've become a hindrance to the spreading of it. You are not allowing others to participate in it. "The Gospel is to be preached, participated in, partaken of, and practiced by every believer." How can that statement be justified? Bear with me for a moment.

A disciple of Jesus, one who loves Him, will keep His commands (John 14:15). Two of those commands are:

> Go into all the world and preach the Gospel to all creation (Mark 16:15).

Go therefore and make disciples of all the nations, baptizing them in the name of the Father and the Son and the Holy Spirit, and teaching them to observe all that I commanded you (Matt 28:19, 20).

To argue that these commands are exclusive to a particular subset of believers is to hinder the propagation of the Gospel and the participation in it. Being a disciple of Jesus necessitates the communication of His Good News.

The making of disciples was accepted as the norm for individuals outside of the church's institutional jurisdiction from the very beginning. There is an inescapable and trans-generational logical loop in the Great Commission whereby it applies to every believer. The most natural interpretation of Matthew 28:19, 20 seems to indicate that all believers are commissioned (delegated) and empowered to make disciples by the propagation of the Gospel.

Furthermore, the church cannot separate Matthew 28:19, 20 from Mark 16:15. The taking of the Gospel to all of creation in Mark 16:15 is encapsulated in the word "Go" of Mathew 28:19. "How beautiful on the mountains are the feet of the messenger who brings good news, the good news of peace and salvation, the news that the God of Israel reigns!" (Isa 52:7). The preaching of the Gospel makes disciples (Acts 14:21).

There is, in the participation of the Gospel, a common unity (community). The church is a body made up of various parts (1 Cor 12:12). The parts can have diverse and specific functions (Rom 12:4), but Paul writes the following to the Corinthian church, "Now if the foot should say, 'Because I am not a hand, I do not belong to the body,' it would not for that reason stop being part of the body. And if the ear should say, 'Because I am not an eye, I do not belong to the body,' it would not for that reason stop being part of the body" (1 Cor 12:15-20 NIV).

One thing often overlooked in this passage is that every part has a voice. The foot has a mouth. It has a voice. Even the ear, the part used for listening, "speaks." No one in the church should be silenced when it comes to the transmission of the Gospel. The church's corporate voice and life are to vividly portray the Gospel to the world. God's intention is to show all of creation His plan for cosmic reconciliation through the making of new creatures (2 Cor 5:17, Gal 6:15), the reconciled body of believers in Jesus (Eph 3:9-11).

THE BLESSINGS OF THE GOSPEL

In his first letter to the Corinthian church, Paul writes, "I do all things for the sake of the Gospel, so that I may become a fellow partaker of it" (1 Cor 9:23).

It would be better rendered in English, "I do all things for the Gospel's sake so that I can be a fellow partaker with you." Paul gets a bad rap for not being humble, but this passage suggests otherwise. Paul didn't "do" these things for himself. He didn't do them for some earthly advantage. He didn't do them to gain favor among men. He sought no honor or applause for himself. Paul did these things for the spread of the Gospel and for its greater usefulness among God's people, the people "won" by his use of the Gospel.

One might argue that Paul was not entirely altruistic in this endeavor. After all, he knew that God would reward him for his service. In that sense, I think Paul and we can partake in the blessings of the Gospel. "He who sows and he who reaps may rejoice together" (John 4:36).

It would be prudent at this stage to ask, "What are the blessings of the Gospel?" In answering that question, I'd like to suggest these, from Isaiah 9:1-6:

- *Light.* People who walk in darkness and dark lands will be enlightened (9:2).

- *Multiplication.* The Gospel restores the Genesis trajectory to "be fruitful and multiply." It multiplies the nation / Kingdom of God (9:3).

- *Joy.* Gladness or joy shall be experienced in three ways: a general sense or feeling, a heightened perception of God's presence, and tangible fruitfulness (9:3).

- *Liberty.* Freedom from burden, ungodly discipline, and oppression (9:4).

- *Victory.* Through grace to every believer (9:5).

- *Christ.* "For a child will be born to us, a son will be given to us; and the government will rest on His shoulders; and His name will be called Wonderful Counselor, Mighty God, Eternal Father, Prince of Peace" (9:6).

The church becomes the people of God by the Gospel. As the apostle says, "Some of the branches were broken off, and you, being a wild olive, were grafted in among them and became partaker with them of the rich root of the olive tree" (Rom 11:17).

And more concretely in Ephesians 3:6, "to be specific, that the Gentiles are fellow heirs and fellow members of the body, and fellow partakers of the promise in Christ Jesus through the Gospel."

Let's take a closer look at this:

- Fellow heirs
- Fellow Members of the Body
- Fellow Partakers of the Promise

- In Christ Jesus
- Through the Gospel

I can't help but repeat those points in succession over and over again and meditate on them. I think that these five mission momentums would activate a livelier Gospel proliferation, sift out hindrances to the spread of it, and act as markers or course correctors along the way.

ENGENDERING MUTUALITY

> But we endure all things so that we will cause no hindrance to the Gospel of Christ (1 Cor 9:12).

The word "endure" in this passage means to suffer all things without complaining, to conceal (literally, "hold as a watertight vessel") any stress put on the container (us) caused by strenuous circumstances. The same Greek word is used in 1 Corinthians 13:7, "endures all things." The Gospel is a message of love and hope, and therefore is characteristically loving and hopeful.

The church gives no cause for offense in anything, so that the mission will not be discredited (2 Cor 6:3). I replace the word "ministry" in this passage with "mission" for two reasons:

They are the same word in the Greek: *diakonian.* It means active service, done with a willing and voluntary attitude. Specifically, it refers to Spirit-empowered service guided by faith or the Lord's genetically encoded persuasion in the newly created believer (2 Cor 5:17).

The word "ministry" is laden with divisiveness. It tends to divide secular and sacred, holy works from everyday life, etc. It also divides people. Ministers become a privileged class within the church and the common or mediocre tasks are left to everyone else. The word "mission" is more inclusive. The church doesn't have a mission to be doled out by the few; the Mission has a mutually active church.

Mutuality and endurance are key components for unity. Unity is crucial for the spread of the Gospel. "Above all, you must live as citizens of heaven, conducting yourselves in a manner worthy of the Good News about Christ. Then, whether I come and see you again or only hear about you, I will know that you are standing together with one spirit and one purpose, fighting together for the faith, which is the Good News" (Php 1:27 NLT).

The church is the artery or living conduit for the Gospel. Division, impatience, exclusivity, and other unBiblical forms of sectarianism contribute to plaque build-up, or clogged arteries, that impede the movement of the body and the delivery of the Gospel. In the Biblical era, Hebrew Christians who were wavering in their faith saw the results of a disjointed people attempting to deliver the Gospel.

> For good news came to us just as to them, but the message they heard did not benefit them, because they were not united by faith with those who listened (Heb 4:2).

Mutuality in sacrifice, service, support, and sent-ness demonstrates a church that is for the furtherance of the Gospel.

THE MESSAGE AND MISSION

That the Scriptures, "the logos incarnated textually" (Clement) should be the source and authority of the Gospel message and mission is a given. But, it's obvious from Scripture that there were, and are "other Gospels." The grace of God birthed in the Galatian church via the Gospel quickly became toxic by the forceful insemination of an anti-Gospel. In addressing them, Paul says:

> I am astonished that you are so quickly deserting the one who called you to live in the grace of Christ and are turning to a different Gospel which is really no Gospel at all. Evidently some people are throwing you into confusion and are trying to pervert the Gospel of Christ (Gal 1:6-7).

The apostle was consistent on this theme with other regional churches. He told the Corinthian church that there is but one Jesus, one Spirit, and one Gospel to be preached to them, and received by them. They were to give no attention to others who, without cause, would draw them away from the Gospel they first received. As my wife has recently said, "We hinder the Gospel when we don't allow people to accept it as it is and demand that they add our laws/criteria/requirements."

There should be no question that for us, the Gospel comes from, and is confirmed by the written word—the Bible. Many who would want to preach another Gospel based on some existential personal sensibilities should not take offense at the testing and proving of their privately held propositions (Acts 17:11). The truth always sets people free; error always binds. The truth element of the Gospel cannot be deviated from or separated out. One cannot cleave the relational Jesus from His reasonable Gospel as if they were two different things.

Paul tells the Ephesian church that the Gospel is the truth message of their salvation, "In Him, you also, after listening to the *message of truth, the Gospel* of your salvation—having also believed, you were sealed in Him with the Holy Spirit of promise" (Eph 1:13).

Likewise, to the Galatian church, "In Him, you also, after listening to the *message of truth, the Gospel* of your salvation—having also believed, you were sealed in Him with the Holy Spirit of promise" (Gal 2:5 NLT).

And again, to the Colossian church, "Because of the hope laid up for you in heaven. Of this you have heard before in *the word of the truth, the Gospel*" (Col 1:5).

The Gospel is personified. In fact, Paul equates the message of the Gospel with the person of the Gospel. For the saints in Ephesus, Paul says, "In him you also, when you heard the word of truth, the Gospel of your salvation, and believed in him, were sealed with the promised Holy Spirit" (Eph 1:13). Jesus said and showed us that he was the truth, the word, and the Gospel personified. In equation form, it might look like this:

$$Word + words = Truth = Gospel$$

In conclusion, this is not about tweaking, innovating, or nuancing the Gospel message itself. While contextualization is critical in cross-cultural settings, the Gospel is fixed. In other words, the message is the message. How that message is communicated and infused into an environment where it currently does not exist, or one that has been contaminated by an incorrect or incomplete Gospel message, is each local church's challenge. Some are more gifted in conducting the Gospel into those situations than others. This is one reason why the spread of the Gospel is, and always should be, a corporate endeavor. Gospel proclamation is a body task. We are to be an ever-moving "cloud of witnesses" (Heb 12:1; Acts 1:8) for our generation and those to come.

It is important to perform content analysis from time to time to assure that the body is staying true to the Gospel message. This comes with spiritual maturation. "Sanctify them in the truth; Your word is truth" (John 17:17). While we have spent considerable amounts of time honing our Gospel message in the Cloud Forest Region of Ecuador, we have spent more time identifying Gospel impediments within our diverse cultures. The fascinating results are that as we identify those things that impede the Gospel, the message itself becomes clearer.

And so, we are for a church that lets nothing hinder the taking of the Gospel to the ends of the earth and works with all Christians everywhere to make this happen.

ABOUT THE CONTRIBUTORS

CHAPTER 1
A CHURCH THAT HONORS THE TRIUNE GOD

By Bobby Auner

When not bent over a book or discussing theology, Bobby Auner is a licensed plumber at Hutson Plumbing. His plumbing has been showcased on TV networks and can be seen in the houses of affluent people such as celebrities and senators. His work ethic is the model of the verse "do all things to the glory of God." He has been happily married for ten years to Jessica Auner, and together they reside in Savannah, GA with their three children: Isaac, Joshua and Chloe. He writes sporadically on his Deconstructing Neverland blog, loves math, scary movies, and lively online discussion groups.

Bobby Auner can be contacted at bobbyauner.blogspot.com

CHAPTER 2
A CHURCH THAT CHERISHES
JESUS CHRIST ABOVE ALL THINGS

By Edwin Aldrich

Edwin "Pastor FedEx" Aldrich is an urban missionary living in Colorado Springs, Colorado where he works among the homeless and addicted. Pastor FedEx serves as a co-pastor at the Colorado Springs Biker Church and teaching pastor at Set Free Ministries. Along with his wife Karen Aldrich and their four children, Pastor FedEx founded His Urban Presence, an inner city ministry dedicated to incarnating Jesus to those living in the margins of society.

Edwin can be contacted at Urbanpresence.blogspot.com

CHAPTER 3
A CHURCH THAT FOLLOWS THE
LEAD OF THE HOLY SPIRIT

By Chris Jefferies

Chris is retired, but worked as a biologist and later in IT. He lives in St. Neots, a typical market town in eastern England, and is married to Donna. They have two daughters, two sons-in-law, three granddaughters, and a grandson. Chris is in regular contact with other members of the Kingdom locally; there's no organization or structure beyond an open network, a happy family. Other interests involve life and the way things work including archaeology, astronomy, church, family, history, photography, blogging, science, technology, travel, and more.

Chris Jefferies can be contacted at scilla.org.uk

CHAPTER 4
A CHURCH THAT CLINGS TO SCRIPTURAL TRUTH

By Steve Scott

Steve Scott regularly blogs at From the Pew. After a twenty year career in architecture ended with the late 2000's housing crisis, he now works in the process industry in a chemical plant. He lives in California with his wife and three sons.

Steve Scott can be contacted at fromthepew.blogspot.com

CHAPTER 5
A CHURCH THAT HOLDS THEOLOGICAL
CONVICTIONS WITH HUMILITY

By Chuck McKnight

Chuck McKnight is a writer and blogger who is passionate about the Kingdom of God. He lives with his wife Tessa and their two children in Bellingham, Washington. When they're not getting coffee, you'll usually find them in a used book store or a thrift shop. Chuck works as a marketer for Lexham Press, the publishing division of Logos Bible Software. In addition to his personal blog, BeingFilled.com, he runs ChristianBooksFree.com, where he posts daily links to free and cheap eBook deals, along with monthly print-book giveaways.

Chuck McKnight can be contacted at www.beingfilled.com and www.christianbooksfree.com

CHAPTER 6
A CHURCH THAT IS MOST NOTABLE FOR ITS LOVE

By Sam Riviera

Sam Riviera has written the series "Getting To Know Your Neighbors" and "Being the Church" on the GraceGround blog. Sam and his wife are retired and live in San Diego, where they spend time getting to know and love neighbors, the homeless and people they happen across in the course of their daily lives.

Sam Riviera can be contacted through graceground.com

CHAPTER 7
A CHURCH THAT FORGIVES

By Eric Carpenter

Eric Carpenter lives in beautiful Savannah, GA with his wife Alice (also a contributor to this book) and three children. He is employed in the Quality Department at JCB, a construction equipment manufacturer. A former institutional church pastor and missionary to South Asia, Eric now desires to see Christ's church thrive in its simple forms in the Savannah area. When not blogging about church and culture, Eric enjoys running, reading, drinking coffee, and going to the beach with his family.

Eric can be contacted at eric-carpenter.blogspot. com

CHAPTER 8
A CHURCH THAT IS COMPOSED OF PEACEMAKERS

By Arthur Sido

Arthur Sido works in financial services and posts his musings, ramblings, and thoughts on the church, culture, and theology at thesidos.blogspot.com. He is married to his wife of 22 years and is the father of eight children. He lives in Indiana with his family on a small farm raising chickens, hogs, and cattle in spite of a complete lack of experience in farming.

Arthur Sido may be contacted at thesidos.blogspot.com

CHAPTER 9
A CHURCH THAT ACCEPTS SUFFERING
AS PART OF THE CHRISTIAN LIFE

By Eric Carpenter

Eric Carpenter lives in beautiful Savannah, GA with his wife Alice (also a contributor to this book) and three children. He is employed in the Quality Department at JCB, a construction equipment manufacturer. A former institutional church pastor and missionary to South Asia, Eric now desires to see Christ's church thrive in its simple forms in the Savannah area. When not blogging about church and culture, Eric enjoys running, reading, drinking coffee, and going to the beach with his family.

Eric can be contacted at eric-carpenter.blogspot.com

CHAPTER 10
A CHURCH THAT EXHIBITS PERSONAL
HOLINESS AND SELF-CONTROL

By Travis Klassen

A former worship pastor who grew up in the church, Travis has seen a lot from "the inside," and is currently writing a book about his experiences. Travis's blog can be found at www.travisklassen.com. Travis lives life with his soulmate Veronica and their two daughters Topanga & Tehillah, near Vancouver, BC, Canada.

Travis Klassen can be contacted at www.travisklassen.com

CHAPTER 11
A CHURCH THAT IS UNITED IN CHRIST

By Stephanie Bennett

Stephanie Bennett is a university professor in South Florida where she invests much of her time mentoring, loving, and teaching students from a Biblical foundation. In courses as varied as Nonverbal Communication, Rhetoric, Communication Ethics and Digital culture, Dr. Bennett focuses on helping students develop and maintain healthy relationships through strong communication skills, prayer, and fellowship with each other in the Body of Christ. Along with her academic research she has recently published a futuristic work of fiction called Within the Walls. She and her husband of 31 years have raised three children and are the joyful grandparents of five.

Stephanie Bennett can be contacted at wildflowerpress. biz/articles/show/39

CHAPTER 12
A CHURCH THAT RECOGNIZES EQUAL LAITY

By Kathleen Ward

Kathleen Ward combines a background in education, years of experience in church ministry, and an interest in social media to describe and predict future trends in the way we do church, blogging regularly at ChurchInACircle.com. She and her husband Kevin-Neil specialize in setting up safe spaces for interaction and participation to equip, engage, and empower God's people. They live in sunny Perth, Western Australia, with their four children.

Kathleen Ward can be contacted at churchinacircle.com

CHAPTER 13
A CHURCH THAT COUNTS EVERY MEMBER
AS A KEY COMPONENT OF THE BODY

By Alice Carpenter

Alice Carpenter grew up as the youngest of six kids on the island of Puerto Rico, where her parents were missionaries. She went to college in western New York State, and has also lived in North Carolina and in India. She now lives in Savannah, Georgia, with her husband Eric and their three children. She homeschools their two teenagers, teaches piano lessons, teaches at a homeschool co-op, and manages the household. She enjoys reading, playing the piano, singing, and spending time with her family and friends. She reminds herself every day that life is a precious gift from God.

Alice can be contacted at thinkingasawoman.blogspot.com

CHAPTER 14
A CHURCH THAT VIEWS ITSELF AS A PEOPLE

By Brian Swan

Brian Swan is the author of a blog called Allergic to BS, a collection of stories about life within the walls of an institutional church. Brian Swan lives in Crestwood, KY with his wife Kristin, and his two children, Emrick and Carley.

Brian can be contacted at abnormalreaction.wordpress.com

CHAPTER 15
A CHURCH THAT ASSEMBLES FOR
THE PURPOSE OF MUTUAL EDIFICATION

By Will Rochow

Will Rochow is a seminary graduate and former Baptist pastor. After having served in three Alberta churches, he left the traditional, institutional church in favor of a more organic form of Christian fellowship. Will sometimes muses that he is now an "Outlaw Preacher." Will is also an avid motorcycle enthusiast and humorist. Other interests include linguistics, travel, wine making, music, extensive reading and maintaining two blogs. Will and his wife Ginny have been married for over thirty years and have two adult children. They currently reside in southern Alberta.

Will Rochow can be contacted at www.rochow.ca

CHAPTER 16
A CHURCH THAT KNOWS LEADERS
ARE THOSE WHO SERVE OTHERS

By Alan Knox

Alan Knox is a husband, father, and IT manager. He and his family live near Raleigh, NC. While in seminary, Alan developed a desire to understand the church as described in the New Testament. He is grateful to God for those brothers and sisters in Christ who share their lives with him as they help each other follow Jesus.

Alan Knox can be contacted at alanknox.net

CHAPTER 17
A CHURCH THAT GIVES LIBERALLY
AND GENEROUSLY

By Guy Muse

Guy Muse grew up on the mission field as a "missionary kid." For the past 28 years he and his wife Linda have served as IMB-SBC missionaries to the country of Ecuador. Their vision is to see every believer making disciples, every house a potential church, and every church building a house of prayer and a missions training center. Guy and Linda hail from Texas. They have two adult children.

Guy Muse can be contacted at guymuse.blogspot.com

SIMPLE CHURCH: UNITY WITHIN DIVERSITY

CHAPTER 18
A CHURCH THAT GIVES EVERYTHING AWAY

By Keith Giles

Keith Giles was formerly a licensed and ordained minister of the Gospel who left the pastorate to enter full-time ministry as a copywriter for the world's largest technology distributor. He is the author of several books including *The Power of Weakness* and *This Is My Body: Ekklesia As God Intended*. He blogs regularly at KeithGiles.com and is the founder of Pacifist Fight Club.

Keith Giles can be contacted at Keithgiles.com

CHAPTER 19
A CHURCH THAT SACRIFICIALLY
CARES FOR THE NEEDY

By Bonar Crump

Bonar Crump is the author of *Throwing Hammers: Separation of Church and Self*. He is a former General Contractor, CFO, Business Manager, and Logistics Consultant. In 2009, he left behind all manner of turning a profit for the world of non-profit humanitarian organizations. His current beloved affiliation is acting as President of the Austin Chapter of Guardians Of the Children (bikers providing assistance and protection for abused children—www.AustinGOC.com). Living in Austin provides him with a fantastic setting as a runner, Harley rider, and aesthetic. He resides with his wife of 18 years and his 8 year old daughter.

Bonar Crump can be contacted at bonarcrump.com

CHAPTER 20
A CHURCH THAT DIES FOR OTHERS

By Steve Sensenig

Steve Sensenig is the co-host of the podcast "Beyond the Box" (www.beyondtheboxpodcast.com), a discussion of topics related to life outside the bounds of institutional religion. A former pastor, Steve is also a professional musician (www.pianosteve.com) and recording artist (www.worship keys.com), as well as a freelance web application developer. Steve and his lovely wife, Christy, along with their two children live nomadically in a 38-foot motorhome, traveling around the United States.

Steve can be contacted at beyondtheboxpodcast.com

CHAPTER 21
A CHURCH THAT SEEKS JUSTICE

By J. Michael Jones

J. Michael Jones became involved with a parachurch organization as a teenager. He experienced eight years of discipleship training through this organization and studied medicine in preparation for going to the mission field. He met his wife Denise in Abu Dhabi, and later they moved to Egypt. After a difficult experience with his mission board Michael suffered a crisis of faith and returned to the states where he studied under L'Abri Fellowship for ten years. Michael and Denise have five children and presently live in Anacortes, Washington, where he is the director of a chronic headache clinic.

J. Michael Jones can be contacted at evangelicalinthewilderness.blogspot.com

CHAPTER 22
A CHURCH THAT RESTORES DIGNITY
WHERE IT'S BEEN LOST

By Kathy Escobar

Kathy Escobar co-pastors The Refuge, a mission center and Christian community in North Denver dedicated to helping hurting and hungry people find faith, hope, and dignity along-side each other. A speaker, spiritual director, group facilitator and advocate, Kathy is passionate about community, equality, justice, and change in the church. She has written several books, including *Down We Go: Living into the Wild Ways of Jesus*, which is centered on cultivating incarnational community in a wide range of contexts. She lives in Arvada, CO with her husband and five children.

Kathy Escobar can be contacted at kathyescobar.com

CHAPTER 23
A CHURCH THAT KNOWS ETERNAL LIFE
IS BY GRACE ALONE THROUGH FAITH ALONE

By Jeremy Myers

Jeremy Myers is an author, blogger, and former pastor. He left pastoral ministry to follow Jesus into the world, and soon found himself led into some dark places where people knew nothing of God's grace and forgiveness. He writes about some of this on his blog at TillHeComes.org, where he also asks difficult questions about Scripture and theology. Jeremy has written eight books, many of which he gives away for free on his blog.

Jeremy Myers can be contacted at tillhecomes.org

CHAPTER 24
A CHURCH THAT SEES EVERY CHRISTIAN
AS A BROTHER OR SISTER

By Christopher Dryden

Christopher Dryden is a lover of words and regularly blogs at damancd.wordpress.com. He has been involved in a number of church initiatives including a church plant. Passionate about conveying who Jesus is and how that affects all of life, he loves using words to help to that end. He lives a fulfilling life ably assisted by not drinking coffee and disliking cheese. He enjoys a good sense of humor and has a deep love for seeing people fulfill their potential. He lives in Stoke-on-Trent, England, with his beautiful wife and three daughters.

Christopher can be contacted at damancd.wordpress.com

CHAPTER 25
A CHURCH THAT PROCLAIMS THE TRUTH
OF THE GOSPEL IN AN UNDERSTANDABLE WAY

By Jeremy Myers

Jeremy Myers is an author, blogger, and former pastor. He left pastoral ministry to follow Jesus into the world, and soon found himself led into some dark places where people knew nothing of God's grace and forgiveness. He writes about some of this on his blog at TillHeComes.org, where he also asks difficult questions about Scripture and theology. Jeremy has written eight books, many of which he gives away for free on his blog.

Jeremy Myers can be contacted at tillhecomes.org

CHAPTER 26
A CHURCH THAT TAKES THE GOSPEL
TO THE ENDS OF THE EARTH

By Miguel Labrador

Miguel Labrador is a missionary in the Andes Mountains Cloud Forest Region of Ecuador. He and his wife serve in that culturally diverse context as mission planters by making disciples of Jesus and bringing the Gospel to where the Lord directs. Miguel blogs regularly at God Directed Deviations (PathwaysInternational.org), is an adjunct professor of Missiology and Ecclesiology at Seminario Noroccidente (Northwest Seminary), and is regularly engaged in local and regional fellowships. Miguel coined the word "Missiorganic," and strives to bring the best of organic and missional church into practice.

Miguel can be contacted at PathwaysInternational.org

23775626R00160

Printed in Great Britain
by Amazon